TRANSFORMATIVE
Education

Valerie Vanyo Ritland

Minnesota State University-Moorhead

Relationship Based Collaboration
with Parents and Colleagues

Kendall Hunt
publishing company

Cover © Shutterstock.com

Kendall Hunt
publishing company

www.kendallhunt.com
Send all inquiries to:
4050 Westmark Drive
Dubuque, IA 52004-1840

Published in the United States of America

Dedication

I wish to dedicate this book to my children, Trevor, Brad, and Tracy Ritland. May you always be grateful for your blessings and mindful of those less fortunate. Use your gifts to serve the Lord, and in doing so, you will find great joy and peace. It is my hope that as a working mother, you always saw that aside from God, you came first in my life.

About the Author

Dr. Valerie Ritland

Dr. Ritland grew up on a small farm in northern Minnesota, with six brothers and two sisters. Valerie attended Moorhead State University, where she received her bachelor's degree in special education in 1976 and her master's degree in special education in 1991. Twenty years later, in 2011, Dr. Ritland received her doctoral degree in educational leadership from North Dakota State University.

Photo Courtesy of Tim Ritland

Through the course of her education career spanning over 40 years, Valerie has worked as a special education teacher, a Head Start Administrator and Consultant, a Pre-K–6th grade principal and is currently teaching as an Associate Professor at Minnesota State University Moorhead (MSUM). One of the classes that Dr. Ritland teaches at MSUM focuses on *building partnerships and collaborating with parents and other professionals.* This class fits well into the passion and core values that Dr. Ritland has for parent–teacher–school partnerships, and the extensive research on parent–teacher partnerships that she has completed. Dr. Ritland has spoken at three international conferences on her parent involvement research, one in Turkey, one in Hawaii, and one in Greece.

About the Contributors

Dr. Marci Glessner

Dr. Marci Glessner has been an educator for over 25 years—with experiences ranging from teaching second grade in an elementary school, working as a K–6 Reading Specialist, a K–5 Special Education teacher, a preschool–grade 6 librarian, and a professor of literacy and special education. She currently teaches at MSUM, located in Moorhead, Minnesota, and lives in Fargo, North Dakota, with her family.

Photo Courtesy of Marci Glessner

Dr. Courtney LaLonde

Dr. Courtney LaLonde earned her PhD in teaching and learning with a teacher education emphasis from the University of North Dakota. Currently, she is an Assistant Professor of Curriculum and Instruction in the School of Teaching and Learning at MSUM. In her present position, she teaches online graduate education courses. She is a former teacher of middle and secondary level Spanish and English learners, and also has experience teaching education foundations courses at the undergraduate level. Dr. LaLonde stays connected to PK–12 classroom practice through her work in mentoring novice teachers. Her most recent research focuses on teacher inquiry/action research, collaborative practices, and learning environments.

Photo Courtesy of Marci Glessner

Introduction

I grew up on a small farm but in a large family with six brothers and two sisters. The spring, summer, and fall seasons were busy times for our family, and everyone played a role in the farm work, gardening, and housework. No one was too small for a task, and it was in this setting that we all developed a strong work ethic and a sense of the power of trusting relationships and collaboration. In spite of the workload of farming and the number of children in our family, my parents did value our education, attended our school activities, and encouraged us to do our best work.

As I grew older and contemplated what to do with my life beyond high school, I felt drawn to the profession of teaching. My decision to pursue special education was, in part, influenced by my youngest brother Kevin, who has Down's syndrome. With few, if any, women in my family who graduated from college, I became an insecure trailblazer. My insecurities were fed by years of negative feedback from some of my teachers, and this became a significant obstacle for me to overcome in my 1st year of college. Thankfully, the work ethic nurtured by my parents would become my means of survival.

In my first special education teaching position, I quickly learned of the value of connecting and collaborating with parents and with my colleagues. Near the end of my 1st year of teaching, as I reviewed the progress that was made by the children who were in my classroom, there was a distinct difference in the range of growth reflected in the reassessment of my students. Although some of my students grew significantly over the school year, other students' gains were minimal. Was my instruction inadequate? Were the children's needs so vastly different? With careful consideration, I surmised that one real possibility was the level of parent involvement of the children I served. Although some families were involved in supporting their children's education, others were merely recipients of what I had to offer their child during the course of the school day. My conclusion was that parent involvement made a significant difference. On the basis of this self-discovery and the impact of my parents' encouragement throughout my elementary and high school education, I became passionate about the value of parent partnerships and collaboration.

I continued to work as a special education teacher for 3 years, and then I was hired as the parent involvement co-ordinator for Head Start. Although I came by the philosophy of parent partnership naturally, my 20 years of working with the Head Start program rooted deeply this value. I witnessed and was an intimate party to the many remarkable stories of children and families changed, because of the parent–teacher partnerships formed.

As Head Start staff, we worked to connect families with the necessary resources available in the community. When we could assist them in meeting their basic needs, families were more ready to focus on their family relationships, school relationships, and their personal growth as parents and providers. It was clear to see that we helped many families understand the value of their involvement with their child's education. Their experiences in Head Start helped to prepare them for their partnership role as their children moved on into elementary school years. Unfortunately, as they moved on, they often returned to let us know that they either did not feel welcomed in the elementary schools or experienced a cultural disconnect to their new environment, and therefore their parent involvement diminished or ended. I have often wondered if that is, in part, why research findings show that the positive impact of Head Start on a child typically washes out by around second grade. In order to sustain that growth, we must sustain the partnerships with parents.

After 20 years with Head Start, I became the principal of a Pre-K–grade 6 private school. For the next 8 years, it was within my power to shape the culture of our school environment. I carefully pondered what a school environment, based on the value of strong parent involvement, would look like. I frequently asked my teachers, "if we know that partnering with parents has a positive impact on the student, socially, emotionally, and academically, what is it that we are willing to do to work with parents?" The parent-focused school setting we created led to the growth of our enrollment, high academic achievement in our students, and some impressive accomplishments within our school and community.

I now teach a building partnerships class at my local university, where I have an opportunity to share my stories of the power of parent and community partnerships. It is my hope that these stories and the activities that I now share in this book will nurture the passion of a new generation of teachers who are even more aware of what can be accomplished with relationship-based collaboration. May this book inspire you to open your heart to a true parent–teacher partnership, and to free yourself of the need for control and power. In doing so, may you be truly blessed with the rewards that you, your parents, and your students are sure to discover!

Dr. Valerie Vanyo Ritland

Acknowledgments

I feel blessed to have grown up on a farm in northern Minnesota. I am proud of my Bohemian and Czechoslovakian heritage, and the many traditions that were passed down from my grandparents. My parents and grandparents modeled a strong work ethic and a strong faith, which served us well through the ups and downs of our childhood.

I feel blessed to have experienced the life of a country school student in a one-room K–grade 8 school house, where I shared my grade with just one other student. The feeling of "family" in that school setting and the remarkable education with such limited resources is an affirmation of what can be done with simple determination and hard work.

I feel blessed to have been a part of such a large family, to have six brothers, two sisters, and the hundreds of cousins who were and still are a part of such wonderful memories in my life. Love, laughter, and hugs were abundant in our family, and became gifts to my children and grandchildren as well.

I feel blessed to have experienced the challenges and the tragedies in my life: death, addictions, and poverty have all helped to build the strength of my character. They have helped me to support others who experience similar life experiences. These challenges have also helped me to appreciate the people and the blessings that I do have in my life every day.

Therefore, I wish to acknowledge the contributions to my life by

1. my grandparents, Dell and Emma Slyter, and Andrew and Anna (Yurko) Vanyo;
2. my parents, Ethel (Dolezal) and Anthony Vanyo;
3. my siblings, John, Darrell, Mark, Cindy, Phillip, Bridget, Terry, and Kevin;
4. my husband, Tim;
5. my teachers, the good ones and the imperfect ones.

A special thank you to my amazing colleagues Dr. Marci Glessner and Dr. Courtney LaLonde, whose expertise in the area of differentiation added greatly to the credibility of content in the final two chapters in this book. Their wisdom and their enthusiasm for this project helped to motivate me as the author, to do my very best work. I am truly blessed to work in the midst of just magical minds and such caring hearts.

Table of Contents

Parent Involvement Versus Parent Partnerships

This chapter helps to define the difference between parent involvement and the more desired system of parent *partnerships*. This chapter will help you to better understand the following:

- Legal and organizational position statements supporting parent involvement
- Rationale for partnering with parents
  - Research-based benefits for
    - Child
    - Teacher
    - Parent
- Risks and challenges of parent partnerships
- Parent involvement versus parent partnership
- Parent partnership strategies
  - Developing an action plan for parental partnerships

LEGAL AND ORGANIZATIONAL POSITION STATEMENTS SUPPORTING PARENT INVOLVEMENT

In the early 1800s, education was primarily provided at home. Formalized education was afforded to only the wealthy or to those of the religious life in order to read the Bible and preach the Gospel (Anderson & Pavan, 1992). During the time of the Industrial Revolution, public education outside of the home became more common and teachers were considered the specialized experts. This made sense at the time because often the children in school were being educated at a much higher level than the educational level of the parents. In the late 19th century, a number of organizations began to form that would study educational practices. It was then that the philosophy of teachers and parents working together would emerge (Berger, 1991). It was a logical conclusion that if parents and teachers were working together it would be beneficial to the student performance. Since that time, a number of laws and organizations would recognize the value of this partnership.

The Title One Law of the Elementary and Secondary Act of 1965 was written to ensure all children, but particularly disadvantaged children, would receive a high-quality education in order to achieve proficiency on state academic assessments. The Department of Education would recognize in Section 1001 (12) of this Act, the value of the role of parents in the academic achievement of children by mandating that schools afford parents *"substantial and meaningful opportunities to participate in the education of their children."* For those receiving Title One services, collaborating with parents was no longer an option; it was an expectation. Another legal mandate for collaboration came in 1975 with the passing of PL-94-142, the first civil rights law for children with special needs. PL-94-142 would ensure all students, no matter what their disability, would be entitled to a free and appropriate education, in the least restrictive environment. The law had six components and one of them was the expectation that parents would be at the table as active decision makers and coeducators of their child. Since this law only mandated shared power for parents of children with special needs, and the special education teacher was the case manager for all children with special needs, most general education teachers during this time maintained their professional boundaries with parents. It would take some time before the expectation of parent partnerships and shared power would trickle down into the general education classrooms and the school culture as a whole. These two laws likely contributed significantly to the merging of parent–teacher boundaries, simply because of the undeniable positive impact the partnership had on the overall performance of the child.

Head Start, which began as an eight week summer program in 1965, was also targeted to assist the disadvantaged. Head Start was formed on the premise that the parent is the primary educator of their child, and therefore one of the four main components of the Head Start program is parent involvement. Designed to break the cycle of poverty, Head Start was focused on collaboration with families and the community, providing decades of research that substantiated the powerful impact of parent–teacher partnerships. This research affirmed that when parents are involved in the education of their child, their child will do better socially and academically in school, and beyond.

In the 1980s, armed with the evidence of the positive impact of parent–teacher partnerships, many professional organizations began to promote parent involvement. Some of those organizations promoting parent participation included the Department of Education, the National Association for the Education of Young Children (NAEYC), and the Council for Exceptional Children. The NAEYC, in its 1997 revised edition of *Developmentally Appropriate Practice in Early Childhood Programs* (*DAP*), identified five dimensions of best practice. "Establishing reciprocal relationships with families" was considered one of the five areas of best practice (Bredekamp & Copple, 1997). The 1997 edition of *DAP* would go on to define several strategies and guidelines on how to effectively and respectfully work with families. These guidelines reference shared knowledge, responsibility and decision-making, regular two-way communication, family involvement in assessment and goal setting, and collaboration and consultation with other agencies that might benefit the family or the child. The strong stand that not "the" NAEYC had taken in recognizing and promoting parent–teacher partnerships was abundantly clear.

After 30 years of research on the impact of parent–teacher partnerships, the National Parent Teacher Association (PTA) formed a position statement surmising parent–teacher partnerships as *transformative*. They would further state that parent–teacher partnerships have a greater impact on student achievement than any other educational reform or strategy (National PTA, 2000).

BENEFITS OF PARENT–TEACHER PARTNERSHIPS: CHILD OUTCOMES

Over 50 years of research have documented the benefits of family involvement and parent–teacher partnerships. Multiple studies have confirmed a number of positive outcomes for children including better test scores and grades, more positive self-esteem, a more positive attitude toward school, and a greater likelihood of graduating from high school and attending college (Epstein, 2001; Henderson, Mapp, Johnson, & Davis, 2007). These results are evident across all socioeconomic statuses and ethnic backgrounds and are not dependent on the educational level of the parent. In other words, the more parents are involved, no matter what the background of the parent, the more positive the impact it will have on the child (Henderson & Mapp, 2002). Although these positive student outcomes should be enough to motivate any teacher to find ways to build strong relationships and partnerships with parents, we should not fail to carefully consider the benefits to the parents, teacher, and school as well.

BENEFITS OF PARENT–TEACHER PARTNERSHIPS: PARENT–FAMILY OUTCOMES

It is easy enough to see that the busyness of our daily lives has created an increase in the stress that parents might experience daily. Often both parents are working, and children have a plethora of options for extracurricular activities to consider. Long workdays, after-school activities, unemployment, military deployments, drugs and alcohol use, and the pressures to make ends meet or climb the corporate ladder have created a lot of stress on parents. The research on how this stress impacts children will be discussed further in chapter 7. What teachers should ponder is whether or not they are contributing in any way to the stress that families might encounter. When teachers operate from a sense of superiority over the parent, this can create a sense of insecurity and families may be stressed or simply avoid contact with the teacher. Furthermore teachers have expectations about what parents *should* be doing, or what they *didn't* do, these perceptions can become judgments that impact the relationship with the parent. If, however, teachers are intentional about building relationships with parents, and value their knowledge and role in the education of the child, then this can result in many positive outcomes for parents.

The first positive outcome might be that parents have a feeling of comfort and sense of peace and trust in the teacher. Involved families do tend to have a more positive view of the school and therefore are more likely to comply with teacher expectations (Epstein, 1995).

According to multiple studies (Bauch, 2001; Epstein, 1995), families benefit from parent partnerships in the following ways:

- Families who are involved have a more positive perception of the school and will more likely follow up on teacher suggestions or requests for support.
- Families will become more knowledgeable regarding what is happening in the school and with this awareness become stronger allies of the teacher and the school.
- Families who are involved tend to become more knowledgeable about child development and appropriate expectations. When parents and teachers respect each other's expertise, the parent is more likely to be open-minded about different ways of seeing things.
- When families are involved, they have a greater insight into what is going on in school so that they can reinforce that at home.
- When parents feel respected and have developed a relationship with the teacher, they will more likely feel comfortable asking the teacher for insight or suggestions for things that the parent might be struggling with at home. Although the teacher should not become the counselor, they should be armed with a great deal of information about resources in the school and the community which can address the needs of children and families.
- Strong parent–teacher relationships tend to reduce family stress and increase parenting skills.

BENEFITS OF PARENT–TEACHER PARTNERSHIPS: TEACHER–SCHOOL BENEFITS

In just a sampling of research studies (Henderson & Berla, 1995; Jordan, Orozco, & Averett, 2002), schools that were surveyed reported the following benefits to their teachers and their school as a whole:

- Teachers felt less isolated and more appreciated.
- Building relationships with the family helped them to better understand the needs of the child and therefore helped them to become more effective teachers.

- Building relationships with the family helped the teacher to be more empathic and effective in working with the family.
- Building relationships and forming partnerships with the parents resulted in more parent volunteers and more support for the teacher and the school.
- Building relationships with the families led to greater involvement and advocacy for the school in the community.

Some evidence of the benefits for the school might be when parents self-advocate for programs within their school, when they look to the city to address issues of safety, when they raise money for scholarships, and so forth. Parents can also provide valuable insight into the search for new curriculum materials, the development of policies, and the hiring of school personnel.

RISKS AND CHALLENGES

With ample evidence to substantiate the rationale for parent–teacher partnerships, one might assume that all teachers would work diligently in building relationships with families. This is not necessarily the case and there are contributing factors that may explain why we do not do as well as we might in this regard.

- The concept of parent partnerships must be a culture that is established by the leadership within the school and the district. This issue will be discussed further in chapter 6.
- Not all teachers are trained in how to work effectively with parents. Although this concept has become more visible in our university teacher preparation programs, the extent to which this concept is covered may vary.
- There may be teachers who have been in the profession for years and did not receive the training that is now more available. If they find satisfaction in teaching without the strong ties to families, they may not see the value in making any changes in this area.
- With the reward comes the risk. Not all teachers feel comfortable with opening their doors to visitors, or sharing what they do with families, out of fear of being criticized or judged. That can and does happen when parents overstep their boundaries. A colleague of mine once said to me when dealing with an overzealous parent, *"sometimes I wish that I was teaching in an orphanage."* Teachers may occasionally encounter conflict and challenges when you work toward shared power and a true sense of partnership, but confident teachers, who are teaching from a place of identified theory and best practice, and who can count on administrative support, will find that there are far more rewards than challenges.
- We are becoming a much more diverse country. The number of immigrants and refugees that we now serve in our schools may require more than simply an adoption of the philosophy of parent–teacher partnerships. We must provide a deeper level of training in how to effectively and respectfully work with families who do not share our language or our cultural values. School leadership must ensure that their staff are adequately trained and that teachers are authentically embracing the diversity of the families that we serve. Political views or cultural bias cannot excuse teachers from embracing all children and families in their classroom. School leadership must model this welcoming spirit and be prepared to provide the necessary training to all faculty and staff in the district.

REFLECTION

Administrators

- Describe and outline how you have created a *culture* of welcoming parents in the school. How do you model the value of parent partnerships to your staff?

- What could you do better in cultivating a community of shared power and parent partnerships within the school?

- What additional training might your faculty and staff need?

- Develop an action plan to identify your goals in working toward strengthening parent partnerships and identify the training and resources that might be necessary to meet your goals. Consider using the Administrative Parent Partnership Assessment and Action Plan as your working tool for goal setting (Appendix A).

Teachers and Resource Staff

- If you know that partnering with parents benefits the child, parent, and teacher, what are you willing to do?

- Write two goals for how you will work to build partnerships with parents, and outline the steps you will take to assure you will meet your goals. Consider using the Faculty/Staff–Parent Partnership Assessment and Action Plan as your working tool for goal setting (Appendix B).

Admin/faculty reflection

- A true partnership with parents means you recognize their expertise and you are willing to share power. What expertise can your parents bring to the table?

- How can we create a reciprocal relationship where we give to the parents as much as we expect of them?

- In what ways can parents be involved in decision-making at a broader level than those decisions that impact just their child? What classroom decisions can they be involved in? What school-wide or district-wide decisions can they be involved in?

- How can your parents be your allies in the community? Consider this discussion in developing your goals for parent–teacher partnerships.

PARENT INVOLVEMENT VERSUS PARENT PARTNERSHIP

Knowing that we have decades of research to substantiate the impact of collaborating with parents should motivate us to action. If we really want to maximize the outcomes for students, parents, and teachers, however, we should be mindful of the difference between parent involvement and parent partnerships. The greatest benefit to all parties will occur when we are aspiring to develop parent partnerships. What is the difference? Parent involvement tends to be more one-dimensional. Parent involvement is when our expectations fall heavily on the parent. It is not wrong if we need the parents to bring bars for the bake sale, help fundraise for uniforms, attend the parent–teacher conferences, and help the child with their homework at home. These are fair expectations, and these actions will send a clear message to the child that the parent values the school, their education, and the child's performance. When we function in this zone of "involvement" and not "partnership," however, we are missing out on the parent, teacher, and school benefits that were referenced earlier.

Parent–teacher partnerships function at a much higher level of collaboration. Parent–teacher partnerships might be compared to a marriage partner or a dance partner. The relationship is critical to the success of the marriage or the flow of the dance. Developing a deep, trusting relationship is essential in order to be effective. Both parties have a role and must learn to read each other's signals and to find harmony. If one pushes too hard, the other party may fall. Each person gives something different in the relationship, but what both parties have to offer is equally as important in a healthy partnership.

Consider what expertise parents might bring to the table? How can you access and utilize their expertise? What power are you willing to give up? Just as you might expect parents to realize their responsibility in supporting their child as coeducators of their child, parents might fairly expect that the teacher will find ways to strengthen the role of parents as responsible decision makers for their child and their family.

THE PARTNERSHIP PYRAMID

How do we move from parent involvement to parent partnerships? In order to strategically move in that direction, it may be helpful to recognize that reaching a true parent partnership might be compared to reaching *self-actualization* in Maslow's Hierarchy of Needs theory. There is a first step in the pyramid that precedes all others, and there are necessary milestones before we can reach the top, where we might function as true partners. We must be comfortable with the fact that each family may be at different levels of the pyramid, and as with Maslow's pyramid, not all families will reach the top during the time we have to work with them. What is important is that all teachers start at the bottom of the pyramid because building a trusting relationship is the foundation of all partnerships. From there we will recognize and support where each family is at and work to consistently and linearly take them to the next level of the pyramid (see Figure 1.1). More time will be spent in chapters 2 and 3 on the details of each level of the pyramid.

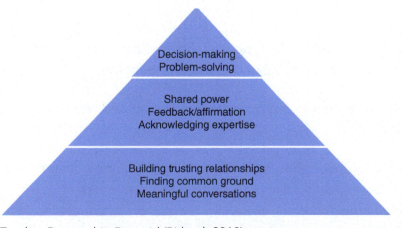

FIGURE 1.1 Parent–Teacher Partnership Pyramid (Ritland, 2019)

PARENT PARTNERSHIP STRATEGIES

Joyce Epstein of Johns Hopkins University has published over 100 articles on the various elements that impact student achievement. One topic that she has many publications on is the impact of family involvement on student outcomes. As part of her research and studies, Joyce Epstein developed six types of parent involvement. Since 2001, this framework has served as a guide in developing school and family partnership programs.

Epstein's framework defines the various types of involvement and presents sample practices that would describe the involvement category more fully. For each category of involvement, you will also see the possible challenges in implementing each type and the potential benefits for students, parents, and teachers. This outline should help teachers and schools to consider how the strategies that they develop might also address the challenges that their practices present.

Although it is important to have an awareness of the different levels of involvement, it may be an unreasonable goal to attempt to involve each family in all six standards of involvement. The higher a family member is on the partnership pyramid, the more likely they are ready for higher levels of involvement. The most important thing is for administration and teachers to have an awareness of the different types of involvement, and to have multiple strategies available at each level of involvement in order to find the best fit for ways that families can use their gifts to partner with the teacher and school.

Joyce Epstein's Framework for Six Types of Involvement

Epstein et al. (2019) describe framework for six types of involvement. These are described in the following sections.

Type One: Parenting

Helping all families to establish home environments to support children as students

Sample Practices

- Suggestions for home that support learning at each grade level
- Workshops, videotapes, and resources on parenting and child rearing at each age and grade level
- Parent education and other trainings
- Family support programs to assist families with health and other services
- Home visits or neighborhood meetings to help families understand school and schools to understand families

Challenges

- Providing information to all families, not just those who can attend the meetings
- Finding strategies for families to share information about their culture, background, and their children
- Making sure all information to and from families is clear and accurate

Results for Students

- Positive personal qualities, habits, beliefs, and values taught by the family
- Balance between time spent on chores, activities, and homework
- Good or improved attendance
- Awareness of the importance of school

Results for Parents

- Build confidence about parenting and child development
- Awareness of own and other's challenges in parenting
- Feeling of support from school and other parents

Results for Teachers

- Understanding families' backgrounds, cultures, goals, needs, and views
- Respect for families' strengths and efforts
- Understanding student diversity
- Awareness of own skills to share information on child development

Type Two: Communicating

Designing effective forms of school-to-home communications about school programs and children's progress

Sample Practices

- Conferences with all parents with follow-ups as needed
- Language translated to assist families as needed
- Weekly or monthly folders of children's work sent home for review
- Regular schedule of memos, phone calls, newsletters, or other communication
- Clear information on all school policies, programs, reforms, and transitions

Challenges

- Reviewing readability, clarity, and frequency of all print and nonprint communication
- Reviewing the quality of letters, newsletters, report cards, and so forth
- Establishing clear two-way communication from home to school and school to home

Results for Students

- Awareness of own progress and action needed to maintain or improve grades
- Understanding school policies on behavior, attendance, and other areas of student conduct
- Awareness of own role in partnerships to ensure informed decision-making

Results for Parents

- Understanding school programs and policies
- Monitoring and awareness of child's progress and responding effectively
- Increased comfort level in communication with school and teachers

Results for Teachers

- Increased diversity and awareness of own ability to communicate clearly
- Appreciation for and use of parent network for communications
- Increased ability to elicit and understand family's views on child's progress

Type Three: Volunteering

Recruiting and organizing parent help and support

Sample Practices

- Parent room or family center for volunteer work, meetings, or resources for families
- Annual postcard survey to identify all available talents, times, and locations of volunteers
- Class parent, telephone tree, or other structures to provide all families with needed information
- School and classroom volunteer programs that provide volunteer options and training

Challenges

- Recruiting so that all families know that their time and talents are welcome
- Creating flexible schedules for volunteers so that working parents can also participate
- Organizing volunteer work; provide training; match time and talents with the school, teacher, and student needs

Results for Students

- Increased learning of skills from volunteer tutoring or mentor support
- Awareness of many skills, talents, occupations, and contributions of parent and other volunteers

Results for Parents

- Understanding teacher's job and carryover of school activities at home
- Self-confidence about ability to work in school and with children to take steps to improve their own education
- Skill development in volunteer work and an awareness that parents are valued

Results for Teachers

- Readiness to involve families in new ways
- Awareness of parent's talents and interests in school and children
- Greater individual attention to students, with help from volunteers

Type Four: Learning at Home

Providing information and ideas to families about how to help students at home with homework and other curriculum-related activities, decisions, and planning

Sample Practices

- Information for families on skills required for students in all subjects for each grade
- Information on homework policies and how to discuss schoolwork at home
- Regular schedule of homework that requires students to discuss and interact with families on what they are learning in class
- Calendars with activities for parents and students to do at home
- Family math, science, and reading activities at school
- Summer learning packets or activities

Challenges

- Designing and organizing a regular schedule of interactive homework that gives students responsibility for discussing things that they are learning in school
- Coordinating family-linked homework activities, if students have several teachers
- Involving families and their children in all-important curriculum-related decisions

Results for Students

- Gains in skills, ability, and test scores linked to homework and classwork, due to more support and increased homework completion
- More positive attitude toward school
- View of parents as more similar to teacher and at home more similar to school
- Increased self-confidence in the student's ability to learn

Results for Parents

- Know how to support and help student at home
- Increased discussion of school, classroom, and homework
- Increased understanding of subject matter each year
- Appreciation of teaching skills

Results for Teachers

- Better design of homework assignments
- Respect for family time
- Recognition of the value of single-parent families, dual income, and less formally educated families in motivating and reinforcing student learning
- Satisfaction and affirmation with family involvement and support

Type Five: Decision-Making

Including parents in school decisions; developing parent leaders and representatives

Sample Practices

- Active PTA/Parent Teacher Organization (PTO) or other parent organizations or committees for parent leadership and participation
- Independent advocacy groups to lobby and work for school reform
- District level councils, and committees for community involvement
- Information on school or local elections for school representatives
- Networks to link all families with parent representatives

Challenges

- Including parent leaders from all racial, ethnic, socioeconomic, and other groups in the school
- Offering training to enable leaders to represent and report back to other families
- Including students (along with parents) in decision-making groups

Results for Students

- Awareness of families' input and power in school decisions
- Understanding that student rights are protected
- Benefits linked to policies that are enacted by parent organizations and experienced by students

Results for Parents

- Inputs into policies that affect child's education
- Feeling of ownership off school
- Awareness of parent's voices in school decisions
- Shared experiences and connections with other families
- Awareness of school, district, and state policies

Results for Teachers

- Awareness of parent perspectives as a factor in policy development and decisions
- View of equal status of family representatives on committees and in leadership roles

Type Six: Collaboration With Community

Identifying and integrating resources and services from the community to strengthen school programs, family practices, and student learning and development

Sample Practices

- Information for students and families on community health, cultural, recreational, social support, and other programs or services
- Information on community activities that link to learning skills and talents, including summer programs for students
- Service integration through partnerships involving school; civic, counseling, cultural, health, recreation, and other agencies and organizations
- Service to the community by students, families, and schools (e.g., recycling, art, music, drama, and other activities for seniors or others)

Challenges

- Solving turf problems of responsibilities, funds, staff, and location of activities
- Informing families of community programs for students such as mentoring, tutoring, and business partnerships
- Assuring equity of opportunities for students and families to participate in community programs or services
- Matching community contributions with school goals; integrating child and family services with education

Results for Students

- Increased skills and talents through enriched curricular and extracurricular experiences
- Awareness of careers and of options for future education and work
- Specific benefits linked to programs, services, resources, and opportunities that connect students with the community

Results for Parents

- Knowledge and use of local resources by family and child to increase skills and talents or to obtain needed services
- Interactions with other families in community activities
- Awareness of school's role in the community and of community's contributions to the school

Results for Teachers

- Awareness of community resources to enrich curriculum and instruction
- Openness to and skill in using mentors, business partners, community volunteers, and others to assign students and augment teaching practices
- Knowledgeable, helpful referrals of children and families to needed services

REFERENCES

Anderson, R., & Pavan, B. N. (1992). *Nongradedness: Helping it to happen.* Lancaster, PA: Technomic Publishing.

Bauch, P. A. (2001). School-community partnerships in rural schools: Leadership, renewal, and a sense of place. *Peabody Journal of Education, 76,* 204–221.

Berger, E. H. (1991). *Parents as partners in education: The school and home working together* (3rd ed.). New York: Merrill.

Bredekamp, S., & Copple, C. (1997). *Developmentally appropriate practice in early childhood education serving children from birth to age 8.* (2nd ed.). Washington, DC: National Association for the Education of Young Children.

Elementary and Secondary Act of 1965: Title One regulations.

Epstein, J. L. (1995). School/family/community/partnerships: Caring for the children we share. *Phi Delta Kappan, 76,* no. 9 (May) 701–712.

Epstein, J. L. (2001). *School, family, and community partnerships: Preparing educators and improving schools.* Boulder, CO: Westview Press.

Epstein, J. L., Sanders, M. G., Simon, B. S., Salinas, K. C., Jansorn, N. R., & Van Voorhis, F. L. (2019). *School, family, and community partnerships: Your handbook for action,* (4th ed.). Thousand Oaks, CA: Corwin Press.

Henderson, A. T. & Berla, N. (Eds.). (1995).*The family is critical to student achievement.* (2nd printing). Washington, DC: Center for Law and Education.

Henderson, A. T., & Mapp, K. L. (2002). *A new wave of evidence: The impact of school, family, and community on student achievement.* Austin, TX: Southwest Education Development Laboratory. Retrieved from www.sedl .org/connections/resources/evidence.pdf

Henderson, A. T., Mapp, K. L., Johnson, V. R., & Davis, D. (2007). *Beyond the bake sale: The essential guide to family-school partnerships.* New York: New Press.

Jordan, C., Orozco, E., & Averett, A. (2002). *Emerging issues in school, family, and community connections.* Austin, TX: Southwest Educational Development Laboratory.

National PTA. (2000). *Building successful partnerships: A guide for development of parent and family involvement programs.* Bloomington, IN: National Education Service.

ACTIVITY

Parent Partnership Plan

- Develop a parent partnership plan using the template provided in Appendix C. Develop at least two strategies in each of the six areas, and identify the preparation or training that will be necessary to successfully implement your strategies.

- Consider how you will address the challenges identified in any of the areas you wish to develop.

Building Meaningful Relationships in Record Time

This chapter will address strategies for teachers that can help you to develop relationships with your students, your parents, and your colleagues in the quickest and most meaningful ways. Upon completion of this chapter, you will be prepared to achieve the following:

- How to build level 1 of the partnership pyramid
  - Strategies to begin *meaningful conversations*
  - Strategies for *finding things in common* with your students and families
- How to use student and parent questionnaires to build relationships
- How to use anecdotal stories and thinking prompts to initiate conversations

LEVEL 1 OF THE PARTNERSHIP PYRAMID: BUILDING TRUSTING RELATIONSHIPS

Meaningful Conversations

Many people have a misconception that all that is necessary to build a relationship with families is to be friendly, and perhaps caring, compassionate, hardworking, knowledgeable, and professional. Truth be told, most of those things are not visible to families or children until we learn to have meaningful conversations with them. To some individuals, having meaningful conversations may come naturally. Still others may have grown up in a home or school environment where meaningful conversations were modeled, and therefore, it is the way they learned to communicate. Many of us, however, tend to spend most of our dialogue with others in friendly conversations that do not build relationships, and therefore our words become wasted opportunities.

A common mistake in how we communicate is what I call, "it's all about me." These are conversations where what I have to say is more important than what you have to say. These conversations tend to focus on what I think you need to know, not what you might want to tell me. They are one-dimensional.

Consider a time when you might have had a conversation with someone when you could scarcely get a word in edgewise. How does it feel when your desire to share or ask something is overrun by the other person's determination to say everything that they need to say as if it was perceived to hold a greater value? If this pattern of communication continues over time, we tend to dread or perhaps even avoid our contact with the offending party. You may think that this method of communication rarely occurs. I would argue that it occurs frequently in the educational arena.

As a teacher we tend to spend a great deal of time *instructing* our students. We lecture, we give directions, and we correct children when they make mistakes. How much of our day is spent in meaningful conversations that help us really get to know the heart of the child? It might serve us well, if we spent the first 3 to 4 weeks of our school year creating the opportunities in our conversations to get to really know our students. That time invested in building a trusting relationship will contribute to our students doing their best work all year long. When we work in the start of a school year to connect personally with each child, that can sustain our relationship for the entire year, and often thereafter. Taking the time to build relationships is what makes a good teacher an exceptional one. The building of positive relationships is what inspires children to make good decisions and to do their best work. The relationships are what children will remember well into their adult years, not how well the teacher knew the content material or what grades they received from their teachers. With core standards and many districts using prescribed curriculum, creating the space and the time to build relationships with our students can be a challenge. Certainly, this challenge can be easily overcome by taking advantage of time before school starts, transition times in the day, playground or lunch supervision time, and scheduling reflection time at the end of each day.

By carefully examining our communication with parents, we might find that one-dimensional conversation is also a reality. In our back-to-school night, we have much that we want to share with the family about our classroom. In parent–teacher conferences, our agenda is often consumed with what we want to tell the parents about the performance of their child, goals you have, and how they can help at home. Our newsletters or handbooks speak at them about the rules, the policies, and the consequences. If we truly measure how much time we spend in speaking *at* them versus seeking their input and their expertise, we may find, at the very least, that there is not a reasonable balance in our relationship. How much time do we spend in conversation with parents to discover who they are as a family? In what ways do we access parents' expertise regarding their child, and their insight into so many other ways that they can contribute to their child, the classroom, and even the school community? When we miss the first step of building the relationship with the child and the family, we are limiting the potential of what we might achieve as true partners. Raising our awareness of creating a better balance in our communication with our students and families is a step in the right direction.

The next step in creating meaningful conversations is to minimize the time we spend in "fluffy" kinds of communication. We often do this as we pass someone in our day, or when we only have a moment to share a few words. "Good morning!" "How are you?" "Isn't it cold?" "Isn't it hot?" "Isn't it a beautiful day?" "I love your coat." "Have a nice day." These friendly greetings might be suitable exchanges when you are at the grocery store with the clerk, or at the post office waiting to purchase your stamps, or when you are passing someone on your way to an important appointment. But if we have learned the elements of meaningful conversations, we can make much better use of our time with students and families even when we are sharing the briefest moments of conversation in our day.

THE FIRST STEP IN MEANINGFUL CONVERSATIONS: GATHERING INFORMATION

The ultimate goal of shared power and decision-making in our partnership pyramid begins with the very basic skill of learning how to engage in meaningful conversations. In order to engage in meaningful conversations, we have to *know* something about the child and the family. Developing strategies that you will use to collect information about the child and the family is a necessary step in creating meaningful conversations. This may be one reason why preschool and kindergarten teachers often have their students create *All About Me* books. It is a starting point to develop meaningful dialogue with the parent and child. Building on the concept of an *All About Me* book may be a very effective strategy for all grades.

Teachers may want to develop key questions appropriate to the age of the grade they are teaching. For first and second grade students, these questions could be posed interview style as the teacher records the student's answers and gives feedback to the child in this exchange. As the students get older, this strategy can be altered a bit to become a student questionnaire that the child fills out at the beginning of the school year. The collection of information regarding the child is meant to be the means to begin meaningful conversations. It is recommended that the teacher present a new set of questions for the student to respond to approximately every 6 to 8 weeks throughout the school year. These questionnaires can become writing assignments so that they are integrated into the daily curriculum. Initial questions should focus on things children enjoy doing, who they spend time with, what they think that they are good at. A secondary questionnaire might focus on what they enjoy about school, what subjects are hard, what subjects are easy, what stresses them, what makes them happy. Teachers must be committed to integrating the information they collect into the dialogue they have with the child and also the parent. It is important to continue to collect information on student perspective and knowledge throughout the year as things can change significantly in a child's life throughout the course of school year.

Teachers can use a similar strategy to get to know the family. Prior to the beginning of the year, teachers could prepare a letter that tells the families a little about who they are as a teacher. Attached to that letter could be a questionnaire that the family would complete and return to the teacher. The family questionnaire would include questions about what the parents know about their child that they would like to share and questions that would help the teacher to know a bit about the family, their culture, and expectations that the parents have for the teacher. Collecting this information is an affirmation of your desire to customize who you are as a teacher, to the needs of all children and families. The questionnaire then provides important information that allows you to begin to have meaningful conversations with families. Bringing this questionnaire to your parent–teacher conference and referencing it in your communication with families will affirm that what they shared was valuable to you. A second-semester updated questionnaire (with different questions appropriate to what more you would like to know about the child and family) can prove valuable as you continue to work most effectively with the individual values, abilities, and expertise of the families you encounter.

THE THREE COMPONENTS OF MEANINGFUL CONVERSATION

Armed with some basic information about the child and the family, you can begin to practice the three main elements of meaningful conversations: *asking questions, connecting or finding something in common*, and *affirmation*. See figure 2.1, Elements of Meaningful Conversations. For example, if children tell you that something that they are good at is playing the guitar, you might ask them how long they have been playing, who taught them how to play, and why they chose to play the guitar. This deepens what you know about their talent and can greatly expand the conversations that you can have with them. You can then connect or find something in common with the children by sharing with them who in your family plays the guitar or what your favorite instrument or music might be.

Affirmation is a very essential component of meaningful conversations, and it is most certainly what builds trust and self-esteem in the child. Congratulating them on their gift, inviting them to play in your class or the school talent show, and encouraging them if they have a higher goal with their musical ability, are many ways that you can affirm what you know is special about them.

The same principles apply to having meaningful conversations with parents. When you know something about the family, you have a starting point for digging deeper, finding things that you have in common, and offering authentic affirmation based on the strengths and expertise that they have shared with you. With the information you have collected, when you see the parents in the grocery store or as they briefly drop their child off at school, instead of the "fluffy" stuff, you can connect to the things that you know about their child and family. The more you engage in meaningful conversations, the more rapidly you will build your trusting relationship so that you can begin to move up the partnership pyramid. When we work to design our dialogue so that meaningful conversations take place, it may seem a bit unnatural at first. Eventually, we will internalize the process and we may find that it improves our relationships with not just students and families but friends, family, and colleagues as well. It is important to remember however, that to build the richest and deepest relationships, we should utilize all three of the elements of meaningful conversations.

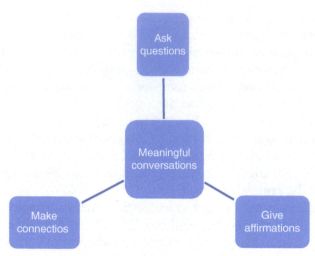

FIGURE 2.1 Elements of Meaningful Conversations (Ritland, 2019)

FINDING COMMON GROUND

Without knowing our students and their families, it will be difficult to find common ground. This is why systematic questionnaires can be such useful tools. A child's file may give you the most basic information, but to connect to their families we need to allow them to tell us things that are important to them. A student or family questionnaire facilitates the beginning of meaningful conversations. Even more importantly, our relationship will move to another level when we *connect* in some manner with the students and families we serve. Knowing a child(ren) can play an instrument, you can invite them to play in your classroom one day. If you or someone in your family plays an instrument, perhaps you can join them one day in song. If a student in your class plays a sport, attend their event and share conversation with them the next day. A parent's place of employment can lead to a conversation about how long they have worked there, and what knowledge or information they might share in the classroom. When you begin to acquire knowledge, you can also begin to connect with children and families. It is beneficial to not only build relationships with your students but also build the relationships within your class and among the families in your classroom. This can contribute to a feeling of being safe and a feeling of belonging to the school family.

In addition to the student and family questionnaires, teachers can create simple strategies of their own to find both simple and significant facts about the makeup of their class. One enjoyable activity is playing *four corners.* In the classroom, teachers can ask students to stand in the corner that best represents the corner they are most aligned with. A safe beginning might be which of the four places you identify would they most like to travel. What is their preferred activity of the options you provide? The *four corner* choices you suggest could also be the subject they find most challenging: math, reading, science, or social studies. When students make choices, all students will find themselves in a spot where others may also be standing. This is a simple way to bond those who often are outliers in the class due to disability or other differences, with others that they might not otherwise bond with. Students enjoy the activity because it allows them to stand, move, and think. When they have found their corner, you can ask them key questions about the choice that they make. This dialogue further educates you about their choices, and when students find things in common with their peers, it can deepen the relationships within the class, no matter how different they really are.

This same activity can be used with parents. Teachers might conduct parent meetings with the families that they serve. How and why would you conduct parent meetings will be discussed further in chapter 4. When you are just beginning to establish a relationship with your families, this

REFLECTION

Building Relationships

- What are some ways that you will build your relationship with students, parents, and colleagues as quickly and as meaningfully as you can?

ACTIVITY

Family and Student Questionnaires

- Develop an initial student questionnaire that you will have students complete in the beginning of the year, and a secondary student questionnaire that you might present and collect after 8 to 9 weeks into the school year.

- Develop a family questionnaire that you will use in the beginning of the school year to help you get to know the child and the family through the parent's perspective.

- Create an action plan that will identify how you will use your student and family questionnaires with your students and with their families.

activity can be insightful. It is a low-risk icebreaker in small or large groups. It allows for movement, laughter, and conversation. Begin with safe questions such as what their favorite food might be: sushi, pasta, burritos, or burgers? How many children do they have: 1, 2, 3, 4 or more? In the beginning, use questions that are safe and playful. Then add the questions that help you to better understand the group of families that you are working with. Examples might be, "how many times have you moved in the last 5 years? 1? 2? 3? 4 or more?" Another useful question for you to ask parents might be, "how would you describe your own school experience? Very positive, mostly positive, both positive and negative, and mostly negative?" These questions are safe enough for parents to respond to because they don't have to say anything; they just have to go to the corner that best fits their experience. Having this insight can provide the teacher with a good perspective of where to start in building their relationships with families and in working with the child.

ANECDOTAL STORIES AND THINKING PROMPTS/ ESSENTIAL QUESTIONS

A day in the life of a teacher is filled with what you have planned and what actually happens. A child asks an interesting question, a student masters a new concept, a troubled child has a trouble-free day, or perhaps you witness a random act of kindness. Every teacher should maintain a journal or a notebook to briefly record these magic moments. When you take the time to write them down, it improves our observation skills. It helps us to see the dispositions of our students and not just the academic performance of a child. Be sure to create a spot or a page for each student in your class so that you are looking for the positive stories and experiences for all. This will give you some content for a friendly note home to parents or something to tell them if you randomly run into them in the community or as they drop off or pick up their child from school. Anecdotal stories are much more powerful than *fluffy* dialogue and they seldom take any more time in our conversation.

Another strategy that can be used in building relationships with students and parents is to have a list of thinking prompts available, until the use of thinking prompts becomes second nature to you. With students you can use these thinking prompts at the beginning of the day or during times of transition. The thinking prompts might be connected to what is happening in the news or what is being discussed in your subject matter. For example, with news prompts you might ask the students to think about the fires in California: What can be done to prevent the fires? What would it be like to have everything you own burn in a fire? What would you do? Regarding subject matter questions, you might ask what they would do to improve our country, if they were president. How can we make our school a healthier place? What can we do to be sure our neighborhoods are safe? These are not necessarily tied to the curriculum that we are teaching at the time, but simply random questions that develop relationships, deepen our thinking, and create problem-solving skills in our students. A teacher might even designate a time during the week for thinking prompts or essential questions. Students tend to look forward to this, and all students can contribute meaningfully to the discussion because there are no wrong answers. This is an esteem builder for those who struggle with confidence or academic performance. For parents, you can send home essential questions or thinking prompts before parent–teacher conferences or parent meetings. Suggestions on conversations parents might have at home with their child can also help to build the relationship within the family. This is especially helpful to parents who perhaps didn't experience meaningful conversations with their own parents as a child.

AUTHOR'S NOTE

The Value of Meaningful Conversations

I have gone to the same hairdresser for over 30 years. I know that I could find cheaper places to get my hair cut. Her salon certainly isn't in the most convenient location for me; there are other shops much closer to my work or home. She knows what can and cannot be done with my thin, fine hair, but I am sure other professionals out there might be able to figure that out over time. The truth is that I am committed to Nan. The single most important reason that I go out of my way to pay more for my haircut is that Nan knows how to have meaningful conversations with me and I enjoy that. Some say that is the gift of a hairdresser. I honestly don't know how she remembers the things that I share with her and then goes right back to a conversation that we had 2 months earlier. The conversations aren't all about me; they are reciprocal. The conversations are not just 30 minutes of the "fluffy" stuff. She remembers my children's names. She remembers that I went on vacation, and where I went. She remembers that I am writing this book. We are not related. We aren't friends, who hang out together or have lunch. But it is just nice to have meaningful conversations when I go to get my haircut. If my relationship with my hairdresser brings me some sense of trust and pleasure, imagine what it would mean to parents to have a safe, trusting, and meaningful relationship with their child's teacher.

ACTIVITY

Thinking Prompts/Essential Questions

- Make a list of thinking prompts or essential questions that you might use with students or parents that might lead to meaningful conversations.

- Create a format for your anecdotal student notes. What is your plan for how you will share this information with parents?

Developing Trust and Giving Affirmation

Trust is a critical element in all relationships. Without trust, a child or parent does not feel safe and secure in fully participating in the relationship or partnership that we wish to establish. In this chapter you will better understand the following:

- What builds or breaks trust
- How to be analytical versus judgmental
- How to gain parent's perspective
- Authentic affirmation
- How to see with the eyes of our heart

If you would . . .
By Virginia Buffett, mother of a son with Autism, 2008

You ask me how you can bridge the future of my children.
You ask how you can form a partnership with my family.
You can start by looking at me as important.
Look past the things that you think you see.

You can start by looking deeper than my social rank in life.
You can start by taking a closer look at me.
When you look at me . . .
What are you *really* thinking?

Do you see my hair in need of washing
or my clothes in need of repair?
Do you wonder why I am nervous and unsure,
As you look down at me, with that condescending stare?

If you step outside your own education,
Put down that pen you hold.
Take my hand and walk with me,
If you would be so bold.

Learn of my own tragic childhood,
Or perhaps just take a peek.
Learn what I did just yesterday,
Or what happened to me last week.

Take the time to listen,
Take the time to see.
Put down your misconceptions,
If you would reach inside of me.

We all come through this life
On both sides of the tracks,
With secrets and temptations
And burdens on our backs.

You made better choices,
And life's road led you to me.
That road leads backwards and forwards
As you can easily see.

If you want to bridge my future,
Then step inside my mind;
For the secret of the future
Is in healing what's behind.

Treat me with some dignity.
And if you would erase my frown,
Try looking up to me
Instead of looking down.

You can unleash the bonds of mistrust,
one tangle at a time.
You could reach within my walls,
If you would brush long past the grime.

My walls are dark and cold.
My heart is encased in stone.
But you could guide me to the light,
If you would leave your own baggage at home.

The message of this poem
Is as clear as it can be . . . .
If you wish to help my child,
Then start by helping me.

BUILDING OR BREAKING TRUST: BEING ANALYTICAL BUILDS TRUST, BEING JUDGMENTAL BREAKS TRUST

Engaging in meaningful conversations and finding things in common with our students and parents are necessary prerequisites to building trust. From there, it is a matter of maintaining a safe and trusting environment. Building trust might happen quickly for some because their life experiences have been more positive. They have learned that they can depend on people and, for the most part, their family, peers, and teachers have proven to be trustworthy. With others, it may take more time to build trust because the significant people in their lives have not been dependable, or have been inconsistent or absent in their support. For these students and families, it is important not to give up. It is important that they get a consistent message from you that you will be there for them, that you will keep your word, and that you will always believe in them, no matter what choices they make. Those who have experienced broken trust in their past will test you, will resist your support, and will make it challenging to continue your efforts to connect with them. Don't give up on them, or you will simply prove that they were right that they cannot trust you either.

What things will break trust in a relationship? One thing that will break trust in a relationship is when we become judgmental. In Virginia's poem she is asking you what you see. Her desire is that you overlook the exterior images and to get to know her story. Can we see with the eyes of our heart? When we know the story behind what we see, we have valuable insight, and that insight can change our vision completely. Virginia, like many parents, has a fear of parent partnership because she has a fear of being judged. I surmise that it may be true that teachers fear partnerships for that same reason. When we have experienced being judged by others, we tend to build a wall to keep people out because we fear that everyone will judge us. If parents and teachers can come to the table as imperfect people with a desire to do good work, only then will this necessary step of trust truly be established, and once it has been established our humanness will not likely tear it down.

Although it is clear that we do not want to judge others, at times, as teachers we do see things that concern us in the students and the families that we work with. Rather than to judge when we find ourselves in these situations, the professional and healthy approach to managing our concern is to be analytical. What can we do to better understand this situation? Does the child or the family need resources to address their situation? Does their situation require any action on my part? If we can keep our mind-set in an analytical mode, rather than a judgmental mode, we will maintain the trust in the relationship that leads to results and not resentment. At any moment if a parent feels judged, we have lost our opportunity to build the necessary relationship that results in positive changes or outcomes. Why would we ever want to do that?

Another action on our part that will quickly break trust is when we fail to do what we had promised a child or a family. It is critical that we keep our word, especially in fragile relationships with others. In the busy days and life of a teacher we may make many promises, and although many of them may be simple, all of them are significant. It can be useful and necessary for teachers to keep an action plan available at all times to keep track of the commitments that we have made to others. At the end of the day, did we keep our word to students and families? This is a good question to include in our daily reflections as we plan for our next day. If we have failed in this regard, and we can immediately address our failure, we can keep intact our trust. This is important for us to be aware of because once we have broken trust, although it might be rebuilt, our relationship is never the same.

GAINING A PARENT'S PERSPECTIVE, AND ACKNOWLEDGING THEIR EXPERTISE

If we are both a teacher and a parent, we can perhaps more readily understand the parent's perspective in the parent–teacher partnership. In what ways are our needs the same and in what ways are our perspectives different? Although we may be able to make some generalizations in this regard, every family is different and therefore our generalizations are not helpful. When we find ourselves in a state of confusion or feeling like we are not certain where a parent is coming from, rather than disengage, we must look deeper. This is a good time to ask ourselves the question that was posed in chapter 1: if we know that parent partnerships are beneficial to the student and the family, what are we willing to do? In some cases, it may be helpful to schedule a home visit, or an extended parent–teacher conference. I am not suggesting waiting until parent–teacher conference time, but are we willing to customize the time we invest in families based on each student and family's needs? If we are not connecting with a family for whatever reason, what else can we try? Will the school district support our reaching out to a family in their home environment or at a place of comfort or convenience to the family, rather than the school building? What questions beyond what we included in the family questionnaire would help us better understand the parent's perspective? Understanding the family culture, the family values, how the family perceives themselves in your partnership may be important areas to explore. Creating a partnership plan for each family that respects the differences and the needs identified by each family, is what we might aspire to accomplish in feeling satisfied that we have addressed the question: what are we willing to do, if we know that parental involvement has a powerful impact on the academic and social development of the child. Giving up on a child or a family, is not an option.

A critical component of an effective working relationship is to gain the perspective of the people we work with. If we are working toward a true partnership, we must also recognize the expertise of the parent and the other collaborating partners that come to the table. In this chapter, we will focus on the parent perspective and expertise, and in chapter 7 we will address gaining the perspective and honoring the expertise of all parties that come to the table.

Teachers often see themselves as educational experts. We may rank our knowledge as having greater power or more value because we have a teaching license or perhaps some experience and some success as a teacher. When we see our expertise as having greater value, we have fallen off the track for experiencing the value of a true family partnership. Our expertise is different. It may even be broader and deeper than that of the parent, but it is not more important.

What expertise do parents bring to the table? Parents have spent more time with their children than we have. They know their children academically, socially, and emotionally. They know what stresses them, what motivates them, how confident or insecure they might be. Yet rather than looking to parents to get their perspective on the strengths and the challenges of their child, we spend the first 8 weeks of the school year trying to understand where each child is at and how to best work with them.

Emily Graham, a senior editor for School Family Media, is a strong advocate for parent–teacher partnerships. She identifies seven things that teachers could benefit from knowing from the parent's perspective. When parents are invited to share this information with the teacher, through document or dialogue, this will help the teacher better understand the child's needs and maximize student outcomes from day one.

1. Does the child have any health needs?
2. Has the family gone through any major changes recently?
3. Does the child have any unique personality or behavioral issues?
4. What are the strengths and the weaknesses of the child?
5. Can the parent tell us anything about the learning style of the child? What stresses and what motivates the child?

ACTIVITY

Analytical Versus Judgmental

- See Appendix E to practice applying the principles of being analytical versus judgmental. Read the scenarios and discuss your honest emotions and reactions. Consider if anything should be done in the situations that are described.

- Discuss any of your own experiences where you have observed a child or family being judged? How could the situation have been handled differently?

- Keep a journal of your observations of how often you make or observe others making judgmental remarks. Is it more or less often than you thought? What strategy will you use when you catch yourself being judgmental?

6. What kind of study habits does the child have? Are there a quiet place and a designated time for homework? Is there an adult to assist with homework when needed?
7. What kind of special interests does the child have? Art? Music? Sports?

These are areas to explore with the parent and when we do so, we are honoring the expertise of the parent. These are easy places for us to begin our partnership and also a place to affirm all that the parent has done to help the child grow, prior to the first day of school in our classroom.

AUTHENTIC AFFIRMATION

When we are intentional about developing our relationship with families, we gain insight into how the family functions, the challenges they face, and the expertise that each parent brings to the table. Our *efforts* to build relationships will be visible or invisible to the family, just as they are to a child. The work that we invest in getting to know the family, building trust, and honoring the parent's perspective provides us with authentic evidence of things that a parent is doing that we can recognize and honor. Even if what the parent provides is at the very basic level of what a parent might do for the family, when we see firsthand the obstacles that the parent may have had to overcome to accomplish that simple task that becomes something very significant to acknowledge. Most parents will need to feel a bit of that affirmation before they are able to climb the next step in the partnership pyramid.

What expertise can you recognize? What contributions can the parent make to the partnership you wish to develop? For some parents it may be getting their child to school on time, for others it may be completing and returning all forms and documents on time, and for others it may be advocating within your community for financial support from businesses. Referring to Joyce Epstein's six types of involvement may be helpful to recognize options for involvement and for affirmation.

AUTHOR'S NOTE

Seeing With the Eyes of Our Heart

When I first started my full-time teaching at Minnesota State University Moorhead, I taught many of my courses in the same classroom. This classroom overlooked the campus mall area that was usually busy with students hurrying from one building to the next to catch a class or to find their next meal. Often students would look out the window and notice an old man walking to the library or the union. He had long white hair with a matching shabby white beard. Students would speak of their encounters with the old man, and remarked on the same brown pin-striped suit that he wore every day. They frequently mentioned his wrinkled white shirt, with a missing button that exposed a growing belly. They kept a distance from him in the union or library because the smell of this unbathed man was noticeable and unpleasant. Those who did not know could only wonder who was this old man and why did he come to campus nearly every day? Some may even have feared him and his odd behavior.

I knew this man quite well. His name was Mr. Dill. He was, and still is, the longest serving president of our university. He was the president while I was a student on this campus. He served as president during the unsettling years in the 1970s and managed war protests and civil unrest. He accomplished a great deal during his tenure, and after he retired he continued to walk to campus every day to read, to enjoy the pleasantries of the campus environment, and to visit with other retired faculty.

When we know a person's story, it can change our perspective of who that person is. When individuals on campus came to know Mr. Dill's story, they saw him in a different manner. They were no longer afraid. They no longer judged his appearance. They looked at him now with compassion and respect. Some may even have begun to warmly greet him or tell his story to others.

The very same principle can be applied to the children and the families that we work with. When we get to know a child's story, or a family's story, it is likely to result in a stronger bond, and a great commitment on our part. When we take the time to listen and we develop multiple strategies to get to know each person's story, we begin to see with the eyes of our heart. That is the kind of vision that all teachers should desire.

ACTIVITY

Family Study

- Family study assignment: Interview a family with a special needs' child. Design questions that will help you understand the families' daily routine, along with what stress and challenges them. The rationale for this assignment is to gather information on what the parent–teacher partnership feels like from the parent's perspective.

- Analyze how this family's story/perspective might impact/alter how you work with this family. What did you learn about the parent's perspective on parent–teacher relationships?

- How did gaining parent perspective help you to recognize the parent's expertise and how did this perspective help you find ways to affirm them?

Family Affirmations

- With your peers and/or your administrative team, compile a list of parent actions or contributions that you could affirm.

- Establish a system where you will attempt to seek out the information that would allow you to gather the information and affirm the contributions made by your families.

Understanding Our Gifts and Our Ghosts

Our life experiences are what shape our gifts and our ghosts in the classroom. This chapter will help you to be more aware of what shapes your values and decisions as a teacher and how our life experiences impact our relationships with others. In this chapter you will

- Learn to map our story lines
- Identify our gifts and ghosts that are impacted by our life experiences
- Understand the impact of parental stress on the child
- Recognize why giving simple feedback is not simple

ACKNOWLEDGING OUR GHOSTS THROUGH A STORY LINE

As teachers, educators, parents, and administrators, we must acknowledge that our life experiences are varied. The positive and negative things that we have dealt with in our lives will impact our values, our decisions, and our judgments. In some cases, they may cause us to be closed-minded regarding other perspectives. In some cases, they may cause us to react or overreact emotionally to a situation that others may find insignificant. Even when our life experiences have been nothing but positive, our life experiences can be skewed in a way that causes a bit of shallowness in seeing the full picture of any given situation.

For example, if our parents were supportive and our teachers all had a positive impact on our formative years, we may fail to relate to the student who has been impacted negatively by poor parenting or instruction. On the other hand, when we have grown up in a harsh home environment that has scarred our heart, we may be more judgmental of parents we work with who have a similar harshness in rearing their child. Although we may be more emotionally drawn to the student, we may unconsciously or consciously be relating to the parent in a more critical manner or we might just ignore or avoid that parent entirely. Our emotional reaction may cause us to forgo any effort to form a partnership with that family.

Drawing a story line can help us to identify our *ghosts*. Our *ghosts* are simply the life experiences from our past that still directly or indirectly impact us today. Drawing a story line is being willing to admit that we have baggage. It is also a healthy thing to acknowledge that we are impacted by that baggage. When we become more aware of our baggage, we can be more intentional and strategic in making decisions based on careful thought and not purely on emotion. It is also helpful to consider that how parents react to our efforts to build relationships and partnerships, is influenced by the ghosts they bring to the classroom. It can be comforting to a teacher to consider that when parents react emotionally, it isn't always about what we did wrong but what happened in their own past.

To create a story line, we begin by drawing a line through the center of a piece of paper (in the landscape direction so it will allow for more room). On the left side is the year you were born; on the right side of the line is where we are today. As you look at your story line, consider the events or people that have had a strong positive or negative impact on your life. If a person or an event had a strong positive impact on your life, draw a vertical line upward and mark the year, and put that event on the top side of your story line. Examples of positives on your story line might be your contribution to a winning team, a special teacher who supported you, a special friend who you could trust, a prize of some kind that you won, or a service mission trip. Any person or event that might have had a strong negative impact on your life would go on the bottom side of your story line, with a vertical line that indicates the timeframe for that experience. Examples of things that one might have on the bottom of their story line might be a time when you were bullied, when you were in an accident, a death in the family, a relationship problem, drug or alcohol issues, or a teacher who was not supportive. After you have completed your story line, the next step in this process would be to analyze what if any of these experiences have become *ghosts* in how you relate to others or how you make decisions in your life and in your classroom. Raising our awareness of how experiences from the past do impact our thoughts and actions can lead to more strategic thinking and less emotional reactions as a teacher, partner, or friend.

THE IMPACT OF CHRONIC PARENTAL STRESS ON CHILD DEVELOPMENT

There is a plethora of research that has been conducted over decades that has substantiated the impact of chronic parental stress on the child. The results of those studies identify outcomes that should cause school districts great concern. Children who grow up in environments of chronic stress may be impacted in the following ways:

- Increased chance of obesity
- More likely to have behavior problems in school
- The academic performance may be diminished
- Increased ADHD (attention deficit hyperactivity disorder) in children
- Higher incidence of depression and other mental health problems
- Higher incidence of suicide

What is quite shocking about the research available is that even before the baby is born, if a mother is under chronic stress, there is a genetic imprint on the developing fetus. In other words, the developing brain is impacted by parental stress before they are even born.

This is affirmation that schools might consider playing a role in addressing type 1 of Joyce Epstein's six types of parent involvement, that is to help to establish a home environment that can support children as students. If we have taken steps to get to know the family and, in doing so, we discover the many challenges and stress factors present in the home, a backpack of food,

ACTIVITY

Ghost Grid

■ See Appendix F. Complete your ghost grid with the positive and negative life experiences that reflect your most powerful memories. Consider how your prior life experiences (*ghosts*) may be impacting your actions and reactions today.

REFLECTION

Ghost Grid

■ Having completed your ghost grid, what did you learn about the positive and negative impact of your life experiences?

■ What gifts did your prior life experiences create?

- What hot spots will you be more aware of with regard to your interactions with students, colleagues, and parents?

- Although you may not have insight into the ghosts that your parents might bring to the classroom, how does the ghost grid help you to know that parent reactions or perspectives are likely connected to their own *ghosts* from the past?

or sending home a winter coat with a box of empathy, does not adequately address what a family might really need. Having the necessary school personnel who can follow up with a family with multiple needs is one option. When school resources are not available. teachers should be equipped with the knowledge of community resources that might best meet a families' needs. Schools might also provide classes, information nights, books, and/or videos that can help to educate parents in a way that might address their most challenging issues. If we can break the blocks that build stress in their lives, we create the opportunity for more positive stress-free engagement with their children.

John Medina, author of *Brain Rules: 12 Principles for Surviving and Thriving at Work, Home and School*, states the emotional stability of the home is the single greatest predictor of academic success. This is a powerful insight and it begs the question, if we can acknowledge how significant parental stress is on the child, what are we willing to do to reduce or eliminate that stress? We might also ask ourselves, are we in any way adding to the parental stress with the expectations or demands we impose that they might not be ready or equipped to address?

GIVING SIMPLE FEEDBACK IS NOT SIMPLE AT ALL

At some point in time it will be necessary to give feedback to parents, our students, and perhaps even our peers and superiors. If you consider the emotional trauma that may have scarred the hearts of children or families, or the invisible ghosts that still walk with them every day, it may help us to understand that giving simple feedback is not simple at all. Although there are many helpful books, articles, and guidelines on how to provide effective feedback, none of this is helpful if we are not focusing on the *person* we are giving the feedback to. This is good rationale for why it helps us tremendously to get to know as much as we can about the children and families we work with. We can follow the fundamental rules about how to give feedback, but we must acknowledge that the recipient of the feedback may not model the desired response to what we have to share. Our role as provider of feedback, therefore, becomes multidimensional. In order for our feedback to have an impact, we must be strategic in compiling evidence to substantiate the message we are delivering, give careful thought to the impact our feedback may have on the individual, and then intermittently follow up with the individual to ensure that the feedback feels supportive and not judgmental, and that our feedback results in positive growth and change. Fundamentally, feedback must be systematic and ongoing, until our desired outcome is achieved. Figure 4.2 offers strategies for providing and receiving constructive feedback. Following these strategies will ensure that our feedback will more likely lead to our desired outcomes. Our feedback will also be more effective if we recognize the interdependency of feedback as outlined in Figure 4.1. Providing effective feedback is not easy, but when implemented with strategic planning and review, it provides great opportunity for growth within your team, and feedback will become a practice that students, parents or peers, will not fear.

Seldom will change take place with simply one incident of sharing feedback. Even if the feedback is detailed in writing, the motivation to change and the support and ongoing feedback to nurture that change are often essential. Parents and teachers should not dwell on the resistance we might encounter when giving feedback. Nor should the length of time it takes to see change or the number of times that feedback is given concern us. If the feedback is on target and the goals are within reach, we must remain consistent in our message and our efforts to seek the desired outcomes.

HOW OUR GHOSTS IMPACT THE GIVING AND RECEIVING OF FEEDBACK

Understanding how to give and receive feedback can be useful information to parents, teachers, and administrators alike. Understanding the elements of feedback is an important first step; however,

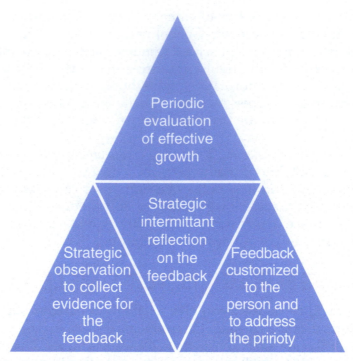

FIGURE 4.1 The Interdependent Elements of Feedback. (Ritland, 2019)

it is even more helpful to remember that our life experiences (our ghosts) are still present and unintentionally they will have an impact on how effective we are in giving and receiving feedback. If we were raised in an authoritarian home or worked in a setting under an authoritarian leadership model, we may have internalized some of the traits of this power-driven model. If we were abused or bullied as a child, we may have acquired the bully mentality in giving feedback or we may have become overly protective and have a difficult time giving any honest feedback that would be addressing behavior that we desire to change. We may even avoid giving feedback altogether. If we had teachers who were not supportive in our school years, we may have a difficult time trusting the feedback from teachers and may get emotional or angry even when the feedback we are giving to a parent or a child is mostly positive. These are the spirits of our ghosts that often overcome the wisdom of what we know is truth. The best that we can do is to commit to internalizing a healthy and respectful process and keeping our ghosts in check when we are givers or receivers of feedback. Being respectful means that no matter who we are giving feedback to, or if we are delivering it face to face, in writing, or anonymously, our words are always meant to help and not to judge.

Another challenging issue with giving and receiving feedback is knowing what to do, or how to react when others have offered feedback to you that was done in a hostile manner, that may have been hurtful rather than helpful, or that may contain content that you feel is not accurate or that you may disagree with. Will you become emotional? Will you be defensive? Will you turn on the person behind closed doors for how he or she treated you? All of those would be human, natural responses; however, they are not helpful to you or the person who has judged you. Be a good listener. Have an open heart to feedback that you disagree with.

There are times when we are not aware of what we do and how others see us. Though our instinct is to provide evidence of why their perspective was wrong, ask for more information regarding feedback given to you that you disagree with. Be willing to be wrong, even if you think you are right. When a parent, child, or boss gives you feedback that you might debate, take it to heart but don't let it brew anger or stress. Give yourself to be mad for a day or a week and then move on. Our mental health is vitally important to be a contributing member of relationship-based collaboration. If, however, our honest efforts to avoid negativity and pessimism cannot be reined in because our

ACTIVITY

Addressing Parental Stress
Teachers and Administrative team activity

To evaluate where your school is at in helping to address and alleviate parental stress, a school may want to ask themselves the following questions:

- What are some of the situations that would contribute to a family's chronic stress?

- What strategies do we currently use to get to know families and to identify families who may be living in chronic stress?

- What resources do we currently have available in our school and in our community to assist families in chronic stress?

- What events, trainings, tools, or opportunities do we currently make available to families that may help to reduce family stress?

Once you have addressed these questions, develop a parental support plan to consider what more you as a school and as a community could do to reduce family stress and help to establish a healthy home environment for parents to be able to support their children and adequately address their needs as a student and family member.

Providing constructive feedback for improvement	Receiving constructive feedback for improvement
Goal: To help one receive information about improving or changing his or her behavior.	Goal: To hear what is being offered nondefensively and to consider feedback as an opportunity for self-improvement. Lundy (1994) noted, "Those who defend their weaknesses will probably keep them: . . . the greatest weakness is the awareness of none."
Be perceptive to the recipient's readiness for feedback. Word your feedback in ways that does not hurt or damage. Identify specific behaviors and situations; be unambiguous and do not generalize. Address behavior and actions, not personality traits. Give feedback promptly: time erodes our memory of events. Make your feedback brief and avoid unneeded repetition. This helps minimize defensiveness. Preface your suggestions with introductory questions: Have you considered? Do you suppose? Would it work? Suggest but do not dictate. Check back with the person on his or her comfort level with the suggestions. Make the person's needs the focus, not your needs as the focus.	Keep your mind pen and listen: absorb as much as you can. Listen for understanding, hold judgment; focus on what is being said. Do not interrupt. Make notes to help clarify your understanding later. Hold your desire to react in check. Take a deep breath. Be quiet and think through your questions. Confirm your understanding of the message with the sender right away. Seek clarification about confusing aspects; request illustrations without being defensive. State your appreciation even if you do not agree: try to regard feedback as helpful insight. Focus on changing your behavior. Seek the assistance of teammates. Ask for feedback on your progress.

FIGURE 4.2 How To Give and Receive Constructive Feedback

Abbreviated and reprinted with permission from Dartnell's T.E.A.M.S.: Together Each Achieves More Success.

work environment is toxic and dysfunctional, in order to maintain our mental health, it may be necessary to find employment in a more supportive work environment. You will be much happier and more effective in an environment where there is commitment to valuing the varied perspectives and expertise that we all bring to the table and where the culture of our school environment is relationship-based collaboration.

LEGAL CONSIDERATIONS TO FEEDBACK

Our society has become much more attentive to the issues of harassment, including verbal, physical, or sexual harassment. Employees, teachers, and parents all have been more vocal in the last few decades about reporting any incidences of misconduct. School leaders must model this in their own behavior and develop policies that would protect students, parents, and teachers from harassment or harm. School administrators must recognize that each school, and each district, has a clearly identifiable *culture* that often becomes their reputation or what contributes to how a school is rated or perceived. That *culture* should clearly model respect, and relationship-based collaboration.

Parents should be welcome in the school but should also be given proper guidance on how to work respectfully and effectively with teachers and administrators. Due to the focus on parent–teacher relationships, it is inevitable that with that parent involvement comes the risk of parents being unhappy with what they see and/or hear. For that reason, there should be written guidance on the proper steps for parents to follow when they wish to address their concerns. First, and foremost, parents should be encouraged to contact the teacher to initiate a meeting. All parents should have the basic awareness of how to exercise this right by informing them of when parents are available for phone calls, or *how* and *when* to utilize school e-mails in establishing an initial contact. A sample written outline of how to raise a question or express a concern in a respectful manner may help when parents' emotions may be elevated. A school social worker or counselor may also be helpful in any meeting that may be requested by the parent to ensure that both parties are able to be heard and respected. The main thing is that all schools consider a well-designed system that guides parents and teachers through the process of conflict resolution. Without a system in place, both parties may be at risk.

AUTHOR'S NOTE

Letting Go

The dean of the college shared this statement with me in a performance review some years ago: *There are only three things that you need to let go of: judging, controlling, and being right. Release these three and you will have a whole mind and the twinkling heart of a child.* I have not been able to track down where this quote came from; however, I have this posted both at home and in my office. These are perhaps the three most difficult things to let go of in our daily lives. But what a weight lifted when we know we are not the judge. What peace and joy we can find in our day, when we let go of control and the need to be right. It took me far too long to learn this, and it is something that we can all work on each day.

Strategically Planning for Positive First Impressions

As teachers we must be intentional about our interactions with students and parents. What is in our heart is not always visible to the families we serve. This chapter will focus on strategies for positive first impressions that can establish the foundation for the relationships and partnerships we wish to establish. You will become more aware of the possibilities of strengthening or creating a plan for the following:

- The power of first impressions
- Being intentional about our first impressions with parents

Why I Hated Meredith's First Grade Teacher: An Open Letter to America's Teachers

by Kylene Beers, abbreviated but not altered

When my first born headed off to first grade, 21 years ago, she held my hand as we walked down the hallway of Will Rogers Elementary School. We walked into Miss Miner's room and Meredith's steps grew more hesitant. This wasn't the … Child Care Center, the place she had gone for years while I was a doctoral student. This place looked different; bigger, more official. There were big-kid desks pushed together in clusters. And though there were centers, they were not the dress-up center or the cooking center or nap center or water play center of the Child Care Center.

The room was filled with children she did not yet know, with books she had not yet read, with a math center that had lost-teeth and birthday charts, and with a big poster by the door labeled, "Our Classroom Rules." "I don't want to stay," she said. I didn't want her to, either. I wanted her still with me, only me. I didn't want to give up those first 6 years of childhood just yet, those years when her world mostly revolved around her parents and new baby brother, and afternoons spent in our local library reading book after book after book, or playing in our neighborhood park, sometimes just sitting on the grass, watching the ants march by. With every ounce of courage, I said, "Oh, you will love first grade. It was my favorite year in school.

I loved my first-grade teacher, Mrs. Allen, and I bet you are going to love Ms. Miner, too." Meredith looked doubtful and so very small. And then Ms. Miner, long blond hair pulled back into a ponytail, saw us, came over, and bent down to Meredith's level . . . Miss Miner was full of energy and excitement. She loved books, wanted to be a great teacher, and had obviously spent weeks making her room look inviting to these 22 six-year-olds.

"Oh, you're Meredith! I recognized you from your picture! Come here and let me introduce you to some others. And let me show you all around the room. And, hey, you brought Corduroy as your favorite book and that's one of my favorite books, too."

And then, somehow, without me even realizing, Meredith's small hand moved from mine to Ms. Miner's and she was gone. She was swallowed up by the sheer joy this other woman brought into her classroom, into learning, and into my child's life. "I guess I'll be going now," I said to Meredith who was busy putting school supplies away in her desk. "So, I'll be just around the corner at our house," I said blinking hard to keep away the tears. I think she nodded. Perhaps she even paused to wave. My feet couldn't move and Ms. Miner gently helped me and a few other moms out of the classroom. "She's really shy," I said to Ms. Miner just as Meredith sped by holding a new friend's hand showing her "all these hooks where we can hang our backpacks."

Meredith was breathless with excitement at the end of that day—every day and by the end of the first week, our family had a new member: Ms. Miner. Each afternoon and for long into the evening, I had to listen to "Ms. Miner said," and "Ms. Miner thinks," and "Ms. Miner showed us," and "Ms. Miner suggested," and when I slipped and said, "Oh damn" at dinner burned in the oven, I was reminded that "Mom, Ms. Miner would never say that." Right, I smiled through gritted teeth. "Ms. Miner says that manners are important," Meredith said, as she explained why we must always put our napkins in our laps, something that I swear I had mentioned a million times.

For the entire year I watched my child fall in love with school, with learning, with figuring out, and most importantly, with her first-grade teacher, Ms. Miner. Meredith, who had once hated ponytails, now only wanted to wear ponytails. And blue skirts, "just like Ms. Miner's." "And Mom, my name starts with an M and Ms. Miner starts with an M, isn't that great!! We match!" Yes, Meredith, just great. Really great. Oh damn.

Though I had been a teacher for years before having Meredith, before sending her off to first grade, I had never truly understood the power of a teacher in a child's life. We give our most precious and priceless to you dear teachers each year, knowing you will teach them, but also hoping you will care for them, help them discover how very much they matter, watching over them, and being there when they have been hurt and then you do just that and they fall in love with you. It shows up in different ways, as they grow older. But it's still there, this deep affection and respect. And, certainly, it's harder to forge those bonds when there are 150 students instead of 22, when the day is fragmented into 45-minute segments, when education seems to be more about the test than the child. But I promise, underneath that bravado of the seventh grader or swagger of the tenth grader you will find that small first grader who wonders, "Will my teacher like me?" And when that child—that teen—knows that you believe he or she matters, then that student will do most anything for you.

To this day, Meredith remembers you, Ms. Miner, and to this day, I so hated how much she loved you that year. And, simultaneously, I am so grateful that she did. As a teacher I am proud to stand beside you in all that you do. But as a parent, well, as a parent I stand in awe of all that you do. And to Ms. Miner, thank you.

THE POWER OF FIRST IMPRESSIONS

Some might say that Ms. Miner simply was an enthusiastic, naïve, and very sweet 1st year teacher who won her students over with her beauty and her charm. But when we carefully examine that first encounter with Meredith, it is clear that the positive first impression was built on strategic planning. Within just a few simple sentences and a short minute, Ms. Miner made a real connection with Meredith. "I recognize you from your picture," an instant connection. "Let me introduce you to some others." She was building her family, bonding them, and ensuring that their first day was a positive one. "And hey, you brought Corduroy as your favorite book, and that's one of my favorite books too." Ms. Miner was affirming her good choice in book, and identifying something that they had in common. In her first encounter Ms. Miner addressed two of the three elements of meaningful conversations, making connections and creating authentic affirmations. These would prove to be powerful actions in the beginning of a positive first impression.

BEING INTENTIONAL ABOUT OUR FIRST IMPRESSIONS WITH PARENTS: THE MILLION DOLLAR MINUTE

Ms. Miner was intentional about her first encounter with each student in her class. She has carefully prepared an enticing environment. She had studied the faces of her children, long before they stepped foot in her classroom. She invited her students to bring a favorite book to class on their very first day. This book was a safety net for them and it also helped Ms. Miner to be able to connect with her students. The five-sentence exchange between her and her students was a Million Dollar Minute. For Meredith and for her mother, that first impression lasted a lifetime.

It can be difficult to predict when we will meet our children's parents for the first time. Will it be at "Back to School" night? Will it be in the hallway of the school? Will it be at the grocery store, when your student tells you, "that's my teacher"? Will it be at parent–teacher conferences? Will it be an unexpected call in the evening at home from a distraught parent we have not yet met face to face? Will it be at a parent meeting, a PTA meeting, or a school event? There will be a different timetable for that first encounter with every family we work with. One thing that we might acknowledge is that we might not be at our best when we are tired and in sweat pants in a grocery store. We might not be at our best when we are called on at home after a long, hard day at work to discuss a matter with someone we have never met. Perhaps we might agree that our first encounter with a parent will likely not be a positive one, if we haven't been strategic in providing opportunities early on and frequently to create a positive first impression. Teachers and administrators who work to strategically plan for first encounters with parents, hold in their hands the power to make the encounters a Million Dollar Minute, which will help teachers float gently over any future conflict that might arise.

FIRST ENCOUNTER

For decades, brides and grooms would avoid seeing each other for the very first time on the day of their wedding until the bride was walking down the aisle. It was considered bad luck to do so. If any pictures were taken, they were only taken of the wedding party or the bride and groom separate from each other. Times have changed and often the bride and groom will have a morning filled with pictures together prior to that march down the aisle. What has remained a Million Dollar Minute, however, is a picture or a video of when the bride and groom see each other for the very first time on their wedding day. This magic moment is called the "First Encounter" picture. The look of the groom when he sees his bride in her gown, and the satisfaction of the bride when she sees the adoring look of her groom, will stand the test of time, as a powerful moment. You could talk on the phone the morning of your wedding, you could tell your groom what your dress looks like and how you are wearing your hair, your best man could tell you how beautiful your bride looks, but the power of this moment is in having the face-to-face encounter.

The meeting of a parent and teacher isn't meant to be a romantic moment by any means, but it should be our hope as teachers, that it is a memorable one for parents. Having a positive first impression is the cornerstone of building a trusting relationship with others. It can be difficult to change how people feel about us, if we get off to a bad start in our relationship.

There are a number of "first encounter" moments that we can create, and in doing so, we increase our chances of the getting off to the best start in our parent–teacher–school relationship. Consider any of the following school activities as the ways and means to create the most powerful "first encounter."

POSSIBLE SCHOOL EVENTS

Welcome Dinner

Families that are new to the school can sometimes find it difficult to feel that sense of belonging and connectedness. This is especially true when families move into districts with children in the upper elementary school years. One strategy to create an early bond between family, teacher, and school would be to hold a picnic dinner in mid-August for new families. This is an opportunity for the school to make families feel welcome, to orientate them to the district policies, and to connect them with more seasoned and involved families. This idea may be the best fit for smaller schools, but bigger schools can find success by holding multiple welcome dinners, in order to keep the evening intimate and engaging. Consider the return on the investment, when districts provide a simple picnic meal, and perhaps a free school logo t-shirt for the student. Families who feel welcome and positive about their child's school experience will likely choose to be engaged in the many other school activities and events that will follow.

If this is your "first encounter" with parents, what will you do to make it a positive experience for them? How will you greet them? What will your agenda consist of to make this a memorable experience for both students and parents alike?

Back-to-School Night

The weeks before the first day of school in the fall can be a very busy time for administration, teachers, and the office staff, with last-minute registrations, class roster changes, supply orders, curriculum planning, lunch payments, and so forth. When staff and faculty are busy, we tend to be task orientated, rather than people orientated. It is important therefore to be mindful of our relationship-building opportunities in the precious encounters we have with students and families in the beginning of a school year.

Most schools do offer some version of a back-to-school night; however, it can often seem a bit chaotic and overwhelming to families. What steps can the school and teachers take to make this as family friendly as possible? If this is your "first encounter" with parents, how can you create some kind of intimacy in the midst of a large crowd of people and commotion?

Class Meetings

Although there may be many school or district events or activities for parents to partake in throughout the year, what could be the most valuable parent–teacher encounter is the one where teachers meet exclusively with the parents of the students in their class. These *class meetings* are best offered two or three times per year. September works well for the first meeting, and January for the second. In a *class meeting*, teachers have the opportunity to help parents better understand teachers' overall philosophy, their teaching practices and management skills, the curriculum, the calendar, but most importantly, how parents can be involved in working with teachers and the school. *Class meetings* should be no more than 75 minutes, and should include time on the agenda for meaningful conversations, question and answer time, and social engagement. In other words, we should be modeling shared power and a reciprocal relationship.

If this is your first encounter with parents, what will you do to welcome them, to connect them, and to affirm them in this experience? What happened in this meeting that will make them look forward to the next class meeting? How did you build trust, and how did you create a safe encounter?

For Your Information/Parent University Nights

One way for school districts to address type 1 of Joyce Epstein's six types of parent involvement is for schools to offer *for your information* (FYI) nights, or *parent university* nights, or whatever term a school might find most fitting to identify an evening when parents can come to receive training on a variety of useful parenting topics. FYI nights, as you might call them, could be offered approximately four times per year. Schools would create a survey that would gather input from parents on what topics they might be interested in, such as managing challenging behaviors at home, creating a healthy balance with the use of technology, protecting our children from bullying, and being educated on the opioid/drug crisis. Primarily, the purpose of these meetings is to strengthen the parent–school relationship and the parenting skills of all families.

What can school personnel do to ensure that the school has impact on empowering parents as decision makers and primary educators of their children? What can school personnel do to ensure that parents who take a risk to participate in these information nights are enriched and affirmed in the role as parent and education partners?

Parent–Teacher Organization/Association

The parent–teacher organization (PTO) or association (PTA) is typically a parent-led organization that exists to support the school in the development of policies and fundraising events for particular functions of the school. Most PTOs or PTAs do have an administrative representative and/or a teacher representative and it is wise to do so to offer some guidance and to keep things on track but not to micromanage the parents and their agenda. What parents do need from the school is good training on their roles and their boundaries, clear expectations, and the regular presence and support of their administrative and/or teacher representative.

There is a risk that PTO/PTA groups can become cliquey and resistant to newcomers whose ideas don't fit with the norm. PTO/PTA meetings can sometimes be a place where diversity in culture or socioeconomic status might lead to some families feeling left out or unwelcome. This was the case when some of our Head Start parents tried to find their way in the elementary PTA/PTO organizations. Many reported that they felt like an outcast. It is important that school personnel are helping to ensure that the supportive environment they are working hard to create, is not derailed by a closed-minded culture within this important organization. When staff help set ground rules with the parents, and those ground rules are reviewed before each meeting, that can help to keep things on track.

Teachers who attend PTA/PTO meetings and grade papers or spend time scanning their phones during the meeting will soon find displeasure from the parents who are working hard on their behalf and on behalf of the school. It is important for teachers to be as attentive to the PTO/PTA agenda as they would expect parents to be when they attend parent–teacher conferences, even if they are only a passive participant.

Meet the Teacher

Developing a relationship early on in the school year is in the best interest of the child, the teacher, and the family. If it nearing parent–teacher conference time, and there are parents whom a teacher has not yet met, the teacher may want to consider holding a "Meet the Teacher" time. Simply set aside a few afternoons in a week where you invite families you have not yet met, to stop by for a coffee/tea chat. It doesn't take a lot of time or cost a lot of money to make someone feel welcome, feel special, and to help them understand how much can be accomplished when parents and teachers are working as partners for the good of the child. If you choose to offer a "Meet the Teacher" time, be sure to have something very simple planned. What can you share about yourself as the teacher? What do you want them to know about who you are and what and how you teach? Perhaps you can some fruit or some cookies to go with the coffee/tea. If you have not planned something simple for this meeting, parents may stop by and be disappointed that they wasted their time.

Teachers must be sure to inform the administration of any plans that they have developed for anything that takes place after school hours. This is to ensure the safety and well-being of the teacher. There are districts who may not approve any after school hour activities scheduled by teachers, in which case the teacher should work with administration to develop time within the school day for this experience.

Parent–Teacher Conferences

There may be few parents who would say that they just "love" going to parent–teacher conferences. If you child has special needs or any challenges in the classroom, these meetings may be dreaded all the more. Parents who have never met the teacher may be especially fearful because they don't know what to expect. Does the teacher really know my child? Does the teacher like my child? Will the teacher support me or judge me as a parent? It is no wonder that some parents are a "no-show" on parent–teacher conference day, and fail to respond when a teacher reaches out to reschedule.

If teachers have reached out to connect with a parent in some capacity prior to parent–teacher conferences, it goes a long way toward reducing the fears of that first encounter. If our "first encounter" took place in another setting and it was a positive and memorable first impression, then our parents may in fact look forward to the parent–teacher conference. But what happens when we come to the table requires strategic thinking and a plan that is designed to meet the individual needs of each family. Parents do not want to feel as if they are experiencing a mechanical encounter with the teacher. If we begin our conferences with a positive anecdotal story about their child (an affirmation of the good job they did in parenting), an overview of what you have planned for the meeting (so there is no hidden agenda items for them to fear), and an invitation to the parent to add whatever is on their mind (a true example that you value their perspective as your partner), there is a good chance that the conference time will go quickly and it will be a satisfying 20 to 25 minutes. What parents do not want to hear in their conference time is, "how tired you are, what a long day you have had, and how you didn't have time for lunch or dinner." They want to hear that you know and love their child, and want to help them to achieve their very best. If there is ever a time when a teacher does not genuinely feel that way, it may be a red flag, and time for some deep reflection on how to regain your passion and compassion.

Other strategies that may help to ensure a meaningful parent–teacher conference might include any or all of the following:

- Send a personal letter to each of your parents, inviting them to the parent–teacher conference. The letter should include the rationale for attending the conference, a brief overview of the agenda, and an invitation for them to send you anything that they would like to add to the agenda.

- Start your conference with an overview of your agenda and the time that you have for your conference. Be sure that anything that they have submitted that they want to discuss is added to the front of the agenda, and that you begin with their questions and concerns. This is a sign that you value what is important to them. Be sure to add more time to your conference if you feel it might be needed. Parents will seldom submit additional agenda items, but they will appreciate and notice that you asked. When they do have an agenda item, it is usually something that is very important to them and they will feel respected and empowered when you address their issue first.

- The practice of including students in the parent–teacher conference is becoming more popular in some districts. It can be effective but only if the students have been well prepared to participate. Another option that teachers could consider is, prior to parent–teacher conferences, plan for brief (5 minutes) conference times with each student to highlight what you plan to share with the parents in the conference. It can also add to the richness of the conference if you ask the students what they would like you to tell their parents in the conference. Adding this element to your conference can also add interest and excitement for the parents to attend their child's conference. Parents are typically excited to see their child's perspective on what they are enjoying about school, what subjects are easy, and what help they might need from their teachers and parents.

■ Parent–teacher conference days are typically long, with back-to-back conferences. Even when we carefully customize each conference to the child and family, we can easily lose track of what we have said, who we said it to, and what promises or commitments have been made. For that reason, teachers can benefit from developing some kind of action plan tool that will track anything that requires follow-up action or simply keeping record of goals or information that was shared. Ideally, this action plan tool could be completed during the course of the conference, and if the teacher had a copy machine in the classroom, a copy could be given to the parent at the end of the conference. You could also use carbonless copy paper as a strategy to record your action items and then share a copy with the parents before they leave. This will help to ensure that teachers and parents both have the same information and that anything that requires action on the teacher's part or the parents' part will not be forgotten. Keeping our promises to families is a critical element of building trust.

■ When parents take the time to come to a parent–teacher conference, it is a sign of their commitment to their child's education. Even if this is the only thing that they have done all year, it is a first step that we can build on. It is an action and a decision that teachers can and should affirm with each parent. Affirmation, as you recall, is a key component of meaningful conversations and building relationships. What if teachers sent home thank-you notes to families after parent–teacher conferences? When we affirm their decision to attend, and draw to their attention why this conference was so important to you and to their child, we will increase the chances of that parent participating in the next conference and perhaps engaging in other ways as well. They will do so because their experience was positive and safe and they were enlightened to the power of the parent–teacher partnership and the impact that has on the total development of their child.

Home Visits

Teachers making home visits to families is not a common occurrence in most school districts. When families are isolated, and have a desire to participate or be involved with the school in some way, home visits might be an idea worth considering. The Head Start program has proven to be effective with their home-based programs or the family visits that most teachers make, because Head Start is a family development program. There are some basic considerations to make if your school requires or supports your making home visits:

1. The home-visit day and time are selected with input from the parent.
2. Home visits should take no more than 30 to 45 minutes.
3. The principal is aware of the dates, times, and families that teachers will be visiting.
4. Whenever possible teachers should not make home visits alone; a paraprofessional, a special education staff, or a social worker, might be a good partner for home visits.
5. Parents should know ahead of time what you will be discussing and who will be joining you.

When this is the only way that a parent and teacher can meet face to face, home visits can provide a great deal of insight into the child, in a few minutes at home. This is a district decision and under no circumstances should a teacher make a home visit without the support and awareness of school administration. Although some parents may fear being judged when teachers come into their imperfect homes, more often, parents feel more comfortable on their own home turf, which can make a home visit a very valuable experience for both the parent and the teacher. Be aware that it is the norm in some cultures, to prepare food for you as a sign of their hospitality and appreciation. It is considered very rude to decline what has prepared for you, so consider at least sampling with great appreciation, what they have prepared.

AUTHOR'S NOTE

What Makes a Difference, When Partnering With Parents?

Administration must be mindful that we must work to form partnerships with all families, not just those with cars and child care. What accommodations are we willing to make to help parents overcome the barriers they might encounter to participate as true partners? In my 28 years in administration, when we worked to remove the barriers, our parent participation was much stronger. As a principal in a small elementary school, I had limited resources, but by creative thinking and being persistent in our desire to solve problems, we always found a way to address most issues that would arise.

As an elementary principal, the two activities that seemed to have the greatest value in my school were the welcome dinner for new families to the school, and the class meetings. Welcome dinners might be more challenging for larger schools, however, it is worth a healthy dialogue to consider the possibility. The class meetings were a great bonding experience not only for teachers and parents but also for parents and parents. One hour of after-school time, twice a year, should be manageable and the reward in how many more parents were involved when we began these class meetings was significant.

Regarding the strategies for parent–teacher conferences, over the span of my three children's elementary and secondary school years, I attended nearly eighty conferences. Not one of the teachers leading these conferences sent me a personal invitation, invited my input on the agenda, or sent me a thank you for attending the conference. I attended them anyway. At times I felt the conferences were meaningful but more often times I felt as if the teacher scarcely knew who my child was. I frequently felt that teachers could do more to cultivate the relationship and the partnership in that precious 20 minutes. Teachers who are open to more strategic planning for their conferences, may be surprised at what differences the strategies can make in our relationships with families.

ACTIVITY

Planning for a Positive First Impression

Develop an action plan with multiple strategies that address the need to make a positive first impression with new students and new families in our classroom/school.

Creating Family Friendly Events

Choose one of the following school events and create an agenda for the event and an action plan of how you will build a positive first impression.

- Welcome dinner

- Back-to-school night

- Class meetings (teacher meeting with parents of students in their class)

- FYI night/parent university night

- PTA/PTO

- Meet the Teacher night

- Parent–teacher conferences

- Home visits

- Create a document that you might use to help your students contribute to the parent–teacher conference agenda. If old enough, the students can be present for part of the conference to share this information directly in the conference. If you prefer, you can collect their input and share the tool with the parents on their behalf. What do children want the parents to know about their school day, their joys, and their struggles and what help they might need from the teacher or the parents.

- Prepare a letter inviting parents to the parent–teacher conference. Be sure to share what happens at the parent–teacher conference, and invite them to contribute any agenda items they might have.

Working With the Differing Needs of Children and Families Who Live in Poverty or Come From Diverse Backgrounds

All teachers will likely work with at least some students who live in poverty during the course of their career. In addition, our country is becoming more culturally diverse and more politically charged, and at times we may be biased toward others who think or act differently than we do. Families have changed, behaviors and violence have escalated, and all of these factors have an impact on how and what we teach in our classrooms. This chapter will help teachers to see the following:

- Families are poor for very different reasons
- Children and families who live in poverty have different needs
- Families who live in poverty may or may not be living in chronic stress
- We *do* need to see the diversity in our classrooms

POVERTY

According to the United States Department of Commerce Census Bureau (2018) in 2017, nearly 40 million citizens in the United States were living in poverty. Families that live in poverty often face the kind of chronic stress that can alter the hippocampus area of the developing brain (Thompson, 2014). The neurological changes in their brain can result in difficulty in controlling emotions, which leads to behavior and relationship problems, and difficulty focusing on tasks, which results in academic and social deficiencies. What is encouraging is that when we intervene early with multiple warm and nurturing relationships, the neurological response to chronic stress can be minimized and, in some cases, reversed. Thompson suggests that children who live in poverty and other forms of chronic stress can and do benefit from healthy interactions from grandparents, teachers, and neighbors. When we take the time to build trusting relationships with our students, we can teach them to be problem solvers and also we can teach them to be resilient in dealing with their own stressors.

If parents have lived in chronic stress throughout their childhood and adult life, it may be harder to change the DNA imprint and the many ways that stress has impacted their life. Reducing their stress by connecting them with needed resources, however, will ultimately reduce the stress at home, which can be significantly important to the development of children at home. We can model how to handle stress and we can be a strong ally in a child's journey through the challenging times in their lives. At the very least, we can work hard not to *add* stress to the daily life of a child or parent we work with. Teachers and schools should be resources that parents can turn to for affirmation and support.

DIFFERENT KINDS OF POVERTY

When we think of poverty and families that live in poverty, we tend to think about Maslow's self-actualization pyramid. We know that children can't learn if their basic needs are not met, and hence that is where we tend to focus our support. Free backpacks with school supplies, Christmas gifts for those in need, winter coats for kids, and weekend food backpacks are given through common programs that are offered now in many schools and communities. Although the kindness of schools and communities is helpful, it does little to actually change the circumstances of the stress that is present when family expenses and needs exceed their resources. Although addressing a family's basic needs may be an important first step, it is dangerous and ineffective to treat every family that lives in poverty the same, because families live in poverty for different reasons as identified in the examples below.

I Am the Single-parent Family

I was in a relationship and I got pregnant when I was 15 years old. I was 16 when my beautiful daughter was born. My boyfriend left me and my parents allowed me to keep my baby and helped me raise my daughter. I did not graduate from high school. I am working as a waitress in the evenings so that my parents can babysit. I am 20 now and I still live with my parents because I don't make enough money to pay for rent, food, diapers, and so forth.

- How might this *single*-parent family life impact the educational needs of a child or put a child *at risk* socially, academically, or emotionally in school?
- What special support, accommodations, or strategies would help the child to do his or her best work in school?
- What challenges does this *single-parent family* have in getting out of poverty?
- What stressors is this family dealing with? Are they living in *chronic stress*? What resources do you think might be useful to this family?
- What would your approach be to forming a relationship with this family and working in a partnership with them?

We Are the Generational Poverty Family

My family has lived on welfare as our primary source of income, for three generations. To supplement the welfare checks, some of my family will steal, sell drugs, or prostitute themselves. Most of my family members have not graduated from high school. Some of my family members are in gangs. One of my cousins was killed by another gang member. Three of my cousins are in jail.

- How might this *projects* family life impact the educational needs of a child or put a child *at risk* socially, academically, or emotionally in school?
- What special support, accommodations, or strategies would help the child to do his or her best work in school?
- What challenges does the *projects family* have in getting out of poverty?
- What stressors is this family dealing with? Are they living in chronic stress? What resources do you think might be useful to this family?
- What would your approach be to forming a relationship with this family and working in a partnership with them?

We Are the Small Farmer Family

My wife and I are 50 years old. We married when I was 22 years old. My father gifted us with some land and we built our own home. My wife and I have nine children. We farmed the land for 37 years with the help of my wife and family. After 4 years of failed crops (due to hail, drought, and wind damage), we were way over our heads in debt and our farm was foreclosed on. Everything we owned was auctioned off. My wife and I have not attended college and our work for the last 37 years has been farming. We don't have another trade and it is hard to find work when you are unskilled and 50 years old.

- How might this *farmer* family life impact the educational needs of a child or put a child *at risk* socially, academically, or emotionally in school?
- What special support, accommodations, or strategies would help the child to do his or her best work in school?
- What challenges does this *farmer family* have in getting out of poverty?
- What stressors is this family dealing with? Are they living in chronic stress? What resources do you think might be useful to this family?
- What would your approach be to forming a relationship with this family and working in a partnership with them?

We Are the Addiction Family

My mother and father are alcoholics. A large number of my aunts and uncles are also alcoholics. My father was emotionally and physically abusive to my mother and to all of us five children. My father blames us for being poor. We are made to do all of the work at home. We are punished severely if our laughter or our conversation wakes my father. We seldom have a regular meal at home. Most of our daily nourishment comes from our school lunches but it can be a very long weekend without a meal.

- How might this *addiction* family life impact the educational needs of a child or put a child *at risk* socially, academically, or emotionally in school?
- What special support, accommodations, or strategies would help the child to do his or her best work in school?
- What challenges does the *addiction family* have in getting out of poverty?
- What stressors is this family dealing with? Are they living in chronic stress? What resources do you think might be useful to this family?
- What would your approach be to forming a relationship with this family and working in a partnership with them?

We Are the Refugee Family

My family escaped the dangers of my country and came to the United States as refugees. In our country we sold our crafts in the streets and grew vegetables in our small garden to feed our family. We often bartered labor for food from those who lived in more affluent means. We do not speak English. My wife and I have an 8th grade education. Our four children did not attend school daily because it was too far to walk to, and at times the children needed to work to contribute to the family income. We are hard workers and grateful people but we are unskilled.

- How might this *refugee* family life impact the educational needs of a child or put a child *at risk* socially, academically, or emotionally in school?
- What special support, accommodations, or strategies would help the child to do his or her best work in school?

- What challenges does the *refugee family* have in getting out of poverty?
- What stressors is this family dealing with? Are they living in chronic stress? What resources do you think might be useful to this family?
- What would your approach be to forming a relationship with this family and working in a partnership with them?

We Are the Medically in Debt Family

My wife is a nurse and I am a teacher. We make a respectable living to support our two children. Everything in our life was going so well for us that our life seemed too good to be true. Our second son was born with spina bifida. We knew before he was born that he had this condition but we had no idea what lied ahead for us and our son. He has had over 40 surgeries and he is only 11 years old. We have over a million dollars in hospital debt. Whenever he has surgery, we must travel over 230 miles to the hospital, which means one of us is with him and one of us must stay home with our other child. It is difficult when your child is having life or death surgery and you can't be there. It is also difficult to take so much time off from work without the risk of losing your job, and the costs for hotels, gas, and food create a rather large burden on our family.

- How might this *healthless* family life impact the educational needs of a child or put a child *at risk* socially, academically, or emotionally in school?
- What special support, accommodations, or strategies would help the child to do his or her best work in school?
- What challenges does this *healthless family* have in getting out of poverty?
- What stressors is this family dealing with? Is this family living in chronic stress? What resources do you think might be useful to this family?
- What would your approach be to forming a relationship with this family and working in a partnership with them?

We Are the Tragedy Family

My husband and I are a middle-income family. We have three children, two in elementary school and one in middle school. We worked hard to save money to buy a bigger home, and just 2 years ago we were able to purchase a bigger home and we now have a manageable mortgage of $200,000. Today, it rained 15 inches in 1 hour and a river of water ran through our home damaging it beyond repair and destroying 70% of our property and possessions. We have no insurance for this type of unexpected disaster.

- How might this *tragedy* family life impact the educational needs of a child or put a child *at risk* socially, academically, or emotionally in school?
- What special support, accommodations, or strategies would help the child to do his or her best work in school?
- What challenges does this *tragedy* family have in getting out of poverty?
- What stressors is this family dealing with? Is this family living in chronic stress? What resources do you think might be useful to this family?
- What would your approach be to forming a relationship with this family and working in a partnership with them?

We Are the Borderline Family

My husband is a high school dropout. My husband has a learning disability that caused him to do poorly in school. His teachers categorized him as lazy and not trying his hardest, which resulted in many angry outbursts and he was inappropriately labeled with an Emotional and Behavioral Disorder. Due to his anger issues and his school struggles, he was bullied for many years as well. I saw how my boyfriend was being bullied and I felt a great sense of compassion for him, which led to our friendship and eventual marriage.

I have attention deficit hyperactivity disorder (ADHD). I did graduate from high school but due to my struggles with staying focused and getting my assignments in on time, I graduated near the bottom of my class. When I took my ACT tests I did not do well because I have a hard time staying on task that long and I suffer from severe test anxiety. Although I had dreams of becoming a teacher, my ACT scores were not high enough for me to get into any college.

My husband and I each make about $10 per hour but we have two small children who need childcare, which we can't afford. Our work schedules must allow for one of us to be at home with the children so we do shift work. We do not have family nearby to help us with childcare.

- How might this *borderline* family life impact the educational needs of a child or put a child *at risk* socially, academically, or emotionally in school?
- What special support, accommodations, or strategies would help the child to do his or her best work in school?
- What challenges does this *borderline family* have in getting out of poverty?
- What stressors is this family dealing with? Is this family living in chronic stress? What resources do you think might be useful to this family?
- What would your approach be to forming a relationship with this family and working in a partnership with them?

We Are the Family With Mental Health Issues

My husband and I married in our mid-20s, and we have three children. I am a social worker and my husband is a skilled carpenter. My husband is bipolar. When he is on his medications, he is functional and can hold a job, but the medications are expensive and my husband doesn't like how the meds make him feel, so he often fails to refill his prescription. He has difficulty holding a job because of his emotional outbursts when he is off his medications. One of his outbursts at work led to him spending time in prison. Now that he is out of prison, it is even more difficult for him to find employment. My job as a social worker does not pay enough to manage our household bills and the regular school expenses of our three children.

- How might the *mental health* issues in this family impact the educational needs of a child or put a child *at risk* socially, academically, or emotionally in school?
- What special support, accommodations, or strategies would help the child to do his or her best work in school?
- What challenges does the *mental health family* have in getting out of poverty?
- What stressors is this family dealing with? Is this family living in chronic stress? What resources do you think might be useful to this family?
- What would your approach be to forming a relationship with this family and working in a partnership with them?

IMPACT OF PARENTAL STRESS ON CHILDREN

Although stress is a constant factor in our lives, one could argue that parents and children seem to be experiencing stressors today that past generations did not face. The pressure to achieve, working multiple jobs to make ends meet, bullying, cyber bullying, drug and alcohol addictions, health and disability issues, refugee and immigration problems, and the overscheduling of activities and homework have resulted in higher levels of stress, anxiety, and mental health issues than ever before. Extensive research on toxic stress has substantiated that parent's stress during pregnancy can even leave a genetic imprint on the fetus, which may result in a higher incidence of ADHD, EBD, and other physical, mental, academic, social, and emotional problems that potentially could last a lifetime.

This knowledge should be significantly important to teachers because it substantiates the need to get to know the families of the children that we work with. If we know what life challenges parents are dealing with, teachers and appropriate school personnel can connect parents with the needed resources to reduce their stress levels. This is not to suggest that teachers must serve as counselors, rather that teachers need to be familiar with the resources within their school and their communities. Knowing the issues that families are dealing with may also help us to know what level of involvement and participation might be the right fit for each family. Having this understanding may ensure that we are not "adding" to the stress that families are managing.

BUILDING RESILENCY IN CHILDREN WHO HAVE EXPERIENCED TRAUMA/STRESS

As we said earlier, the impact of chronic stress or trauma on the mental health and well-being of children can be significant. While teachers may not always be able to significantly change the home environment that surrounds each student, they can help children to be healthy survivors of their life circumstances. Research findings on children who grow up in traumatic or dysfunctional environments, reveal that they do not all suffer with emotional or behavioral problems. Many of these children will actually grow up to be healthy, responsible, and productive citizens. What can make the difference in one child suffering the impact of their childhood, and another child becoming a thriving survivor? The good news, is that we can make a difference in the direction and the decisions that these children will make.

Adults who had traumatic or stressful childhoods and grew up without being impacted socially, emotionally, or behaviorally, attribute that positive outcome to having had at least one loving and supportive relationship with an adult. Often that caring and supportive adult was a teacher who never gave up on them. (Abelev, 2009) This affirms the value of taking the time to build relationships with our children and families.

Janas (2002) and Henry & Milstein (2002) identified four attributes of resilient children. Interestingly, resilient children tend to be socially competent; that is, they are skilled in establishing and maintaining positive relationships with peers and adults. That would not be possible if they hadn't observed or learned somewhere, from someone, what a healthy, respectful relationship looks like. Teachers and schools in general need to see the development of social skills as a primary curriculum objective. Second, resilient children tend to have the ability to problem solve. They have learned or must be taught, where to find the resources and the help that they need. If they are not learning that at home, where else can they learn to problem solve if not in school? Third, resilient children have a strong identity. In spite of what is happening at home or perhaps because of what is happening at home, they develop a sense of autonomy, of self-sufficiency, and self-confidence. Finally, resilient children have clear goals and high aspirations; they see their future as bright. If we as teachers, can help to cultivate these four attributes in all children, we have fulfilled our role in teaching children what is most important and what will help them to become healthy, functioning adults. One could argue that these four attributes might rise above anything else that a child might learn in school. What is your plan to address these attributes?

Ginsburg (2015) identified seven interrelated components that he felt were the fundamental building blocks of resilient behavior. Ginsburg referred to the components as the seven Crucial C's: competence, confidence, connection, character, contribution, coping and control. Many school districts have adopted the concept of building character as a core value. You will often see visual evidence of this character development with posters, pictures or slogans in the hallways of the school. This visual reminder is just a small part of the action that schools must take in order to develop these competencies. It is what happens within the walls of the classroom, however that really matters. How are teachers actually building the competencies that are so important to all children, but especially those who grow up in chronic stress or trauma?

REFERENCES

Abelev, M. (2009). Advancing out of poverty: Social class worldview and its relation to resiliency. *Journal of Adolescent Research,* 24(1), 114–14.

Ginsburg, K. (2015). *Building resilience in children and teens (3rd ed.)* Elk Grove Village, Il; American Academy of Pediatrics.

Henry, D. & Milstein, M. (2002) *Spreading resiliency: Making it happen for schools and communities.* Thousand Oaks, CA: Corwin Press.

Janas, M. (2002). Twenty ways to build resiliency. *Intervention in School and Clinic,* 38(2), 117–121.

BOOKS THAT ADDRESS POVERTY, DIVERSITY, AND PREJUDICES

- *The Absolute True Story of a Part Time Indian, by Sherman Alexie*
- *The Other Wes Moore,* by Wes Moore
- *Just Mercy,* by Bryan Stevenson
- *Killers of the Flower Moon, by David Grann*

ACTIVITY

- Research and identify at least two quality articles on the impact of parental stress on child development. Save these articles as word documents and put them in your resource file for future reference.

ACTIVITY

- Case study: Select one of the families living in poverty from above. Answer the questions that are posed in the text and then construct a family support plan based on the varying needs of that family.

ACTIVITY

- Research the diversity area you would most like to learn about. Prepare a paper or presentation for others based on your findings. Optional diversity topics might include researching countries that represent where our current immigration is coming from, LGTB, the culture of bullying, etc.

ACTIVITY

- Consider the four attributes of resilient children. What strategies will you use to develop these attributes within your classroom?

- Consider Ginsburg's seven components of resiliency. Create a table of how you will address each of these seven components. A sample table can be found in Appendix J.

Creating a *Culture of* Collaboration With Students, Staff, and Professionals

Our partnerships with parents and our students are essential. We must also be mindful of our relationships and the need to collaborate with student and teacher support personnel. This chapter will focus on building healthy and constructive relationships with our colleagues, in order to develop a team approach to supporting the families we serve. This chapter will address the following:

- School culture and leadership
- Transitioning from parent partnership to relationship-based team collaboration
- Team planning and evaluation
- Addressing conflict within your team

SCHOOL CULTURE AND LEADERSHIP

A school district could have buildings filled with teachers who were passionate about parent–teacher partnerships, but their efforts might be in vain if the school leadership does not model a *culture* of *promoting and supporting* those partnerships. Administrative support is more than an encouraging word or a pat on the back for the efforts made by teachers. School leaders are crucial players in relationship-based collaboration. What is practiced by teachers should be modeled by administration. Here is what that looks like from an administrative perspective.

Administration Should Take Time to Get to Know Their Teachers

Just as teachers find ways to get to know the families they work with, so should administrative staff find ways to get to know their teachers. The art of engaging in meaningful conversations begins with learning something about the people on your team. It is in this discovery process that we are then armed with the means to make connections ask essential questions, and then offer authentic and meaningful affirmations. Being a teacher, like being a parent, is a difficult and underappreciated endeavor. Affirmations nurture our confidence and can give us strength and energy to manage our challenges. Affirmations can reassure all parties that we are valued and we are capable.

Environmental Evidence of Parent and Teacher Support

What will the parents see and experience in the school building when they arrive that sends a message that they are welcome? Who is there to greet them warmly and answer their questions? Is the focus solely on checking them in to be sure they are a safe visitor, or have we taken the time to be hospitable as well? Are the principal and other administrative staff ever present in the building at times of the day when children and families are sure to be in the office or in the hallways? Are there signs on the door or in the office to acknowledge that we value the presence of parents in our school? Although school space is often fully occupied, can the school create a space somewhere designated as a parent room, where resources might be available and parents could visit and make connections with other parents? Perhaps there may be times during the month when school board members would be present in the parent room or once a month when the principal or other administrative staff would be available for short periods of time to answer questions or just to develop relationships. Schools might consider creating a parent hospitality plan to ensure that administration and the campus in general have given thought to what they are doing to engage parents.

The effort that administration makes to show their support to the teachers and staff in their building should also be intentional and visible. Every school building has a culture and that culture is created by the leadership within the building, but it is sustained by all. If the administration models respect, hospitality and a positive, professional environment, they should expect and promote these qualities within the building and among those who reside in any capacity within the building. Administration should find ways to celebrate not just the student academic outcomes in their building, but the ways in which they are modeling and therefore teaching how to be a responsible citizen within the culture of the school. Those skills are important and transferrable to the larger community.

Tangible Support for the Teachers to Promote Parent Partnerships

Teachers spend a great deal of time and energy each week preparing the daily curriculum for their students, grading student work, attending meetings and trainings, and doing *other duties as assigned*. If administrators are on board with creating a culture of relationship-based collaboration within their school, they must also be on board with finding ways to open up time in the teacher's week or month to be able to plan for and do the work as outlined in our first five chapters of this book. Teachers need time to make phone calls, send emails, prepare letters, and make themselves available to meet with parents outside of regular parent-teacher conferences. The first step would be for teachers to prepare and present their parent partnership plan to administration. (All teachers should have a parent–partnership plan.) The next step is for the appropriate individuals to be able to find fiscally efficient ways to free up teacher time in order that they can implement their plan. Options might include getting substitute teachers or having teachers of the same grade to partner up. Perhaps twice a month on a designated day, one teacher teaches for all social studies students or math students, and the other teacher is free to work on parent partnership tasks. On another day, the teachers would switch roles. The point is that teachers need to see that they are given the administrative support to create teacher partnerships by supporting strategies that allow the time for teachers to do the work. Even if school districts must set aside some additional dollars for substitute teachers to ensure that the time is there for teachers to work on parent partnerships, the investment will pay back in higher student test scores and stronger parent participation. That would be considered a good investment!

FROM PARENT PARTNERSHIP TO RELATIONSHIP-BASED TEAM COLLABORATION

Thus far, the focus in this book has been on the parent–teacher relationship, but we know that there often times are more than two people on the team. With the integration of children with special needs into the regular education classrooms, the team might also include a paraprofessional,

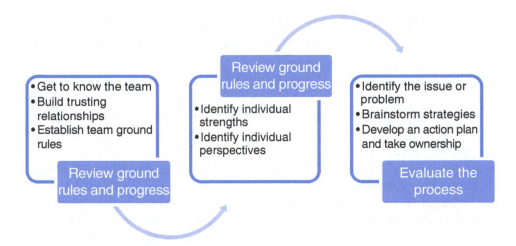

FIGURE 7.1 Relationship-Based Collaboration Model (Ritland, 2019).

a special education teacher, a speech therapist, an occupational therapist, a family advocate, and a school counselor. Each of these professionals comes with their own area of expertise, their own perspectives, their own ghosts, and their own personalities and temperaments. Although the common area of interest is the child, finding common ground is not always as easy as one might think. Collaborative teams might benefit from integrating the Relationship-Based Team Collaboration model shown in Figure 7.1.

Get to Know the Team and the Individual Strengths on Your Team

Ideally, teachers work to get to know the parents and the team prior to coming to the table for the first time to address an issue or a problem. However, even if the teacher knows the other parties at the table, the team also needs to know something about the individuals on the team. Unless we have come to address an emergency issue that is time sensitive, in following the Relationship-Based Collaboration model, the first step will always begin with getting to know and establishing trust within your team. Teachers may have their own strategies about how to establish that trust. One option is to use a simple tool to identify the individuals on the team, what role they play, and what strengths and expertise they might bring to the team. A sample of that document can be found in Appendix G. When a variety of people come to the table as a team, it is especially helpful to use this instrument because parents are often introduced to multiple people within the school and it can be challenging to remember the names and roles of everyone that is present. This can be a document that is completed by all parties and then complied and distributed to all by the teacher or the case manager. This tool is also useful in the forming of school-wide committees that might include individuals who are not familiar to one another.

Establishing Team Ground Rules

For each group of individuals that forms a team, there may be different values that surface as important to the function of the group. There may also be some standards that just make sense to put on the table no matter what the make-up of the team. The purpose of the development of ground rules is to be proactive in discussing things that can become problematic if left unsaid. Ground rules can also help a team to be efficient and productive with their meeting time. Johnson and Johnson (2000) cited the following as more critical rules of conduct:

- Attendance: Starting on time and ending on time
- No interruptions caused by taking or making phone calls except in an emergency
- Everyone participates in discussions

- All members commit to confidentiality; nothing is shared outside of the meeting room
- Shared knowledge: All members share their knowledge so that everyone is prepared to analyze the facts
- All members have a role in the implementation of the decisions that are made

Although these strategies may be a good start to a list of ground rules, the group may decide there are other actions that are important to the team, such as how to handle members who do not comply with the ground rules.

In the Relationship-Based Collaboration model Figure 7.1, you will see that ground rules are reviewed throughout the planning process. A useful strategy may be to add the ground rules to the team profile handout or to add them to the top of every meeting agenda. Doing so will help the team to stay committed to the principals they identified. When reviewing the ground rules on a regular basis, the team begins to function in a less casual and more professional manner and there are times when that is necessary in the partnership.

Gaining Perspective of Individual Team Members

As team members we tend to see the issue, the problem, or the situation only from our perspective, which will reduce our effectiveness as problem solvers. One of the biggest mistakes that we can make is to begin to brainstorm solutions to a problem that is only partially identified. Long before we can begin to problem solve and establish goals and responsibilities, we must take the time to ensure that we have heard and attended to each person's *perspective* of the problem.

Imagine that the district has a problem with bullying in the schools and they have decided to form a committee to address this problem. On this committee, they have gathered the following members: students, parents, teachers, a school counselor or social worker, and the principal. One might think that the problem is clear to everyone: *we have a problem with bulling in our schools.* But if we take the time to listen to each person's perspective, we will be much more effective in solving the issue, because right now we don't know what the problem really is.

Students' perspective might be fear. They are afraid that they might get picked on. They don't know what to do when someone is picking on them, and they don't know what to do if they see another student getting bullied. According to Hawkins, Pepler, and Craig (2001), more than 57% of bullying situations stop when a peer intervenes on behalf of the student being bullied. Therefore, a student's perspective might be, "what do I do when I am being bullied, or one of my friends is being bullied? How do I stay safe?" The parent's perspective might be that there are no consequences for the inappropriate bullying behaviors. Or they might feel that supervision is inadequate in the places where it is most needed, such as the lunchroom and the playground. The teacher's perspective might be that the staff needs more training, or that the school is in need of social skills training materials. The school counselor or the social worker might be interested in working with the parents on teaching responsible behaviors and managing challenging behaviors at home. The administration's perspective may be focused on the liability and budget costs.

The antibullying committee is in need of a good facilitator who is able to draw out the individual perspectives from all parties. When everyone has a chance to explain their concerns and their perspectives, two things will happen. One important thing that happens is that you are able to see what information might be necessary to share or to collect. For example, perhaps a student survey needs to be done to see how many students report being bullied or feeling unsafe. Perhaps the school needs to look at the data on the number of incidents that have been reported in the last year. Perhaps the committee needs to be made aware of the resources that already exist in the school district. Shared perspectives lead to the identification of missing information and ensuring that everyone at the table has the same shared knowledge. The second benefit of taking the time to hear everyone's perspective on an issue is that the committee has a better chance of being more accurate in defining the problem and in finding solutions that are effective in resolving the problem.

Who Is Not at the Table?

In our effort to address issues and solve problems, there are times when our thinking is rather shallow on who to bring to the table. Sometimes it can be helpful to ask, "Who is not at the table that should be here?" In the case of the antibullying committee, could the lunch room staff be helpful in our dialogue? Does the bus driver have useful information and insight? Would a special education paraprofessional or the school secretary have other useful perspectives? There are times when certain expertise is brought in for insight, but they don't necessarily have to be a long-term participant in the process. Always be mindful of who is not at the table.

TEAM PLANNING AND EVALUATION

The parent and teacher partnership can be a powerful and effective team. Teachers will also find it necessary to build relationships and partnerships with many other individuals for the good of the families they serve. Forming partnerships with other key school staff can help to share the load and at times the emotional burden of trying to differentiate for each student and family. Schools may identify particular teams that are meant to encourage team planning and collaboration. One such team that is common in many schools today is the Professional Learning Community (PLC). This team works with a common group of children at a certain grade level. Although this team teaches different subjects to these children, the purpose of this team is share information about how the child is doing in general, and what issues if any a child might have that would require special strategies or intervention. The teachers share strategies and data that are meant to help each child work to his or her potential.

Another kind of collaborative team within the school might be a Response to Intervention (RTI) team. RTI teams tend to meet to discuss primarily children who are in tier 2 or tier 3 of the pyramid, in other words children who need more intensive instruction, specialized instruction, or direct support in order to work to their potential. The RTI team might have regular education teachers, special education teachers, paraprofessionals, counselors, and a number of other specialized staff that would participate in the work of this team. School districts might also have behavioral intervention teams and a variety of other student-focused or school-focused teams.

No matter what the team or committee, in order to function efficiently and effectively, collaborative teams could benefit from an identifiable system of operation. Teams that operate too casually, or that lack a clear identity and focus, will often have frustrated team members, and in some cases teams will eventually just fall apart. When teams fall apart, it can take some effort to pull these team members back in and to rebuild their faith that relationship-based collaboration and committing to being a part of a team can really be worth their time.

Strategies that can keep a team on task and productive include the following:

1. Have a regular scheduled meeting time. Teams that don't commit to regular meeting times will often find it impossible to get their team together. Scheduling as you go or as needed results in calendars that fill with other commitments and presents a challenge each time you attempt to find a common meeting time. In some cases, this may delay the need to act, address, or resolve an issue in a timely manner.

2. Have a clearly identified purpose for your team, and make sure that everyone is orientated to the team function.

3. Seek out diversity in thinking and perspectives for more well-rounded decision-making. Schools can sometimes overlook the value of having a paraprofessional, a parent, or a student representative on your team, when their input can be quite valuable.

4. Have a designated facilitator for each meeting. One of the other duties that might be assigned might be timekeeping. Use the gifts of the team members when deciding on these roles. At times it works best for a consistent facilitator, but other times the team works well when the role of facilitator is rotated.

5. Identify team ground rules and review them frequently. The need for confidentiality in any collaborative team should always be at the top of the ground rule list. How will you address rules that are not followed? Over time, when unexpected problems arise, you may want to add to your ground rules, if necessary.

6. Be sure to have an agenda that is set by the team and distributed in advance of your meeting.

7. Forty-five to sixty minute meetings that are well organized can be very productive. Keeping to that time frame respects the attention span and availability of all parties.

8. At the end of each meeting, evaluate the ground rules and the overall productiveness of the meeting, record any action items, and prepare your next meeting agenda. Be sure to make note of any data, information, or special guests that might be needed in your next meeting. At times a team can benefit from bringing a specialist in who is not ordinarily a part of the team but can help with an issue currently being addressed.

9. Use the consensus model in decision-making, rather than majority rules. The consensus model works toward negotiating a decision that everyone can live with. Consensus decision-making honors the relationships within the team and lends itself to a unanimous effort to ensure successful outcomes.

10. Identify the roles that everyone might play in carrying out any decisions that were made by the team. When everyone is involved in implementing a plan or decision, everyone shares in the celebration of success or shares in the responsibility when our plan didn't work and we need to go back to the drawing table.

11. Trouble shoot any team conflict or dysfunction. When a team does not seem compatible or productive, it is best to pause the process and seek out a suitable resource that can help remediate the conflict. There should be no shame in acknowledging when the team is struggling. It is a sign of professionalism when we decide to seek help, rather than abandon our need to address the challenges that come with our work. Whether it is a team working on a child's Individual Education Plan (IEP) goals, a team working on diversity issues, or a team working on antibullying policies, the strength of our character is often built while working through the greatest challenges in our personal and professional life.

12. Take time to celebrate your good work, but don't *over-celebrate*! When teams *over-celebrate*, the celebration becomes insignificant. It is good practice to share the team accomplishments in each meeting, but a real celebration takes place when something more significant has been accomplished. When teams take the time to get to know each other, they will know what kind of a celebration is meaningful to the members of the team. Perhaps it is a special treat from the bakery, a certificate of accomplishment, a thank-you note from administration, or a temporary break from committee meetings, whatever it is that the team deems as meaningful.

13. Develop some kind of a document that will keep track of the history of your work and a reminder of where you are heading. To some, this might seem too formal and unnecessary; however, without a tool to reflect the history of your work, teams will often waste a great deal of time, trying to remember where they left off. A sample of a team meeting worksheet can be found in Appendix H.

MANAGING AND RESOLVING CONFLICT WITHIN YOUR TEAM

If you have taken the time to get to know your team, established team ground rules that you review on a regular basis (maybe even have them posted on the top of every agenda), worked to understand everyone's perspective, then you have done many things that will help to create trust and harmony within your team. Even when teams have done all the right things, teams can get side-tracked by conflict. Contributing factors to team conflict might be different values, ghosts from our past (as discussed in chapter 4), personality and temperament differences, varying confidence levels, different learning and leadership styles, and political differences.

No collaboration book on any shelf can help us to address that fact that we are different and our differences will sometimes result in conflict within our teamwork. Some will be aware of the conflict within the team and may be stressed, while others may be blind to it. Team members with flexible temperaments will go with the flow. Team members with spirited temperaments may have greater intensity in their responses and discussions. Insecure team members may be reluctant to speak up, or may get defensive if others disagree with their position. When team members aren't following the ground rules, some may feel disrespected and frustrated. For many reasons, we can fall off the track of working in the spirit of collaboration. If, however, we are committed to *relationship-based collaboration*, then we will invest in a periodic evaluation of our teamwork. In doing so, we are affirming that everyone in this team is important, and all perspectives are valued. No one team member has higher power over another. Taking the time periodically to evaluate our effectiveness as a team will also interrupt any bigger issues that might arise when the smaller issues are ignored.

Teams can construct their own evaluation tools or look to the resources available. Teams may want to conduct more frequent informal evaluations and then choose to conduct a more *formal* evaluation of the team using an agreed-upon tool. One sample instrument is available in Appendix I. When the team has completed their evaluation tool, if any team member has concerns about how the team is functioning, they should not be singled out. It may be necessary to bring in a neutral skilled facilitator to address any major issues within the team.

REFERENCE

Hawkins, D. L., Pepler, D. J., & Craig, W. M. (2001). Naturalistic observations of peer interventions in bullying. *Social Development, 10*(4), 512–527.

ACTIVITIES

- Develop team ground rules for any teams you work with.

ACTIVITIES

- Experiment with utilizing the tools in Appendices G, H, and I or create your own collaboration tools.

- Establish the criteria for what you think is important in a collaborative team.

- Evaluate the current functioning of the teams you are a part of including your parent partnerships. Establish goals to consider how to strengthen your team(s).

ACTIVITY

- Case studies on conflict resolution. Discuss real life situations that have happened in your personal or professional life, and consider if relational collaboration or any of the strategies discussed in this chapter might have helped in a peaceful resolution to the problem. If no, why not.

Moving From Collaboration Toward Transformative Teaching

Contributed by Courtney LaLonde
© Kendall Hunt Publishing

A transformative experience is one that causes an important and lasting change. All teachers should aspire to transform learning experiences for their students, but it is not a simple process. Transformative teaching involves creativity and collaboration, in-depth organization, multiple resources, and a focus on the learner. This chapter is written to support teachers in their efforts to prepare transformative learning experiences by

- Providing an understanding of what it means to teach in a transformative learning environment
- Presenting elements that should be considered when planning for transformative teaching

TEACHING IN A TRANSFORMATIVE LEARNING ENVIRONMENT

Much time and effort goes into creating valuable opportunities where students can actively learn. The first step in moving toward transformative teaching is to work at providing a learning environment that is relationship and learner centered. This involves giving thought to the physical design and organization of learning space, functions of the classroom setting, and a focus on the learner.

Physical Design and Organization of Learning Space

When designing and organizing learning space, teachers make decisions on such things as how to arrange classroom furniture, where to set up work space and resource materials, and how to decorate. The physical classroom environment has an effect on students' attitudes and behaviors (Garrett, 2014). The way a classroom is arranged, organized, and even decorated establishes an ambiance that is meant to be conducive to student learning. There are numerous ways to arrange classroom learning space, and teachers should feel comfortable trying different blueprints until they find one that works best for them and their students. Teachers typically inherit physical learning space that comes with limitations; in this case rethinking how the space can be used more effectively is important to provide learners with an environment that is conducive to active learning (Hayes Jacobs, 2010). Some ways of "rethinking" existing space include the following:

- Joining classrooms
- Using empty space in the school building for certain learning activities
- Leaving the classroom for field experiences regularly (not just for special events)
- Providing virtual and Web-based learning experiences

No matter how learning space and resources are utilized, it is important to ensure that there is ample space for student interaction so that peer relationships can develop, as well as room for the teacher to move among students in order to interact with them frequently (Garrett, 2014). Furthermore the classroom setting should provide for six basic functions (Steele, 1973) that are essential to creating a space that will promote learning.

Six Functions of the Classroom Setting

In all reality, teachers and students will spend a large amount of time together in the classroom setting. Each function plays a role in the ultimate goal of engaging students in transformative experiences. The six functions of the classroom setting are (1) shelter and security, (2) social contact, (3) symbolic identification, (4) task instrumentality, (5) pleasure, and (6) growth (Steele, 1973). They can be defined and applied in the following ways (Steele, 1973; Weinstein & Novodvorsky, 2015):

- Shelter and security—students feel safe and secure in both physical and psychological senses
  - Teach proper use of equipment and materials
  - Ensure accessibility
  - Incorporate elements that are "soft" or responsive to touch
  - Provide areas for privacy
- Social contact—opportunities for students to interact with teacher and peers
  - Design learning space that allows for movement, conversation, and collaboration
- Symbolic identification—what the classroom setting says about the teacher's goals, values, and beliefs and the students' activities, backgrounds, and accomplishments
  - Add homelike décor (lamps, pictures, curtains)
  - Display student work—avoid displaying only the very best student work
  - Incorporate materials that reflect the cultural backgrounds, interests, and experiences of the teacher and students, doing so affirms that we value the individuality of our class family
- Task instrumentality—using physical design of space (including placement of resources and materials) to support learning
  - Arrange seating to meet the specific needs of the activity at hand (individual work, group work)
  - Support flow of learning by placing resource materials where they are most accessible to learners
- Pleasure—aesthetic value of the learning space
  - Provide a space that students and the teacher both enjoy being in
- Growth—learning space that invites students to explore, investigate, observe, test, and discover
  - Think about activities that the classroom setting needs to accommodate
  - Create open-ended activities
  - Think about modifications that students might require
  - Consider other adults working in the setting (e.g., paraprofessionals, instructional coaches)

Although there is no one perfect learning environment design, reflecting on the learners in your classroom, *what* you will do and *how* you will carry it out in the learning environment, is an important first step in designing a physical learning environment that focuses on the learner (Weinstein & Novodvorsky, 2015).

REFLECTION

Your Personal Experience

- Think about an educational experience that truly changed you or your way of thinking about something. What do you remember from that experience?

- How did you feel in that moment?

- How were you involved in learning?

- Why do you think this particular experience comes to mind now?

Focus on the Learner

A teacher-centered method of instruction is one in which the instructor transmits knowledge to students. This is a traditional learning environment where students are passive learners; knowledge is acquired outside of the context in which it occurs, as the teacher is the primary source of information. Instruction emphasizes learning right answers, and only students are viewed as learners in the classroom (Huba & Freed, 2000).

In contrast, learner-centered teaching focuses on the construction of knowledge by supporting students in the process of gathering and processing information. The teacher's role is to foster communication, inquiry, critical thinking, and problem solving skills among all learners. Students are actively involved in learning, to the point where they are able to use knowledge to address problems in real-life contexts. The teacher assumes the role of a coach, or facilitator, in a learner-centered environment. Instead of focusing on obtaining the right answers, emphasis is placed on discovery, generating new questions, and learning from mistakes made; this provides students with opportunities to take a more active role in learning. In a learner-centered environment, the teacher and students learn together—collaboration and cooperation which evolve from the relationships developed with the teacher and within the class, are essential (Huba & Freed, 2000). This means that content will be taught in ways that generate interest and promote involvement for all. Planning content with pedagogical approaches in mind is an integral part of focusing on the learners in the classroom, especially those who are diverse in their needs.

Teaching Diverse Learners

The new "norm" for classroom teachers in public schools is a wide diversity of language, culture, and class (Commins & Miramontes, 2006). Varying academic abilities also exist as schools continue efforts to include students with exceptional needs in general education classrooms (Banks, et al., 2005). Teachers must be prepared to work with a diverse group of students that have a wide range of personal and scholastic experiences, as well as varying academic needs (Banks, et al., 2005), if they truly hope to transform learning experiences, with respect for all learners and their individual experiences, a belief that all students can learn regardless of their background, and a willingness to question and change personal teaching beliefs and practices if needed.

It is important for teachers to put forth effort in trying to understand their students instead of focusing on whatever preconceived notions they might have. Trying to truly understand students involves digging deeper to learn about all aspects of their lives, even those that go beyond the walls of the school.

Understanding factors that impact students' lives such as religion, language, relationships, home life, poverty, history, and future goals is extremely important (Finley, 2014). Knowing what is "real" to students and also sharing what is real about yourself will help teachers build relationships and connect to diverse learners on the path to transformational teaching. Strategies that help diverse learners succeed include setting high expectations, using culturally relevant instructional practices, and supporting parent and community involvement in the classroom (Finley, 2014).

Setting High Expectations

It is important to continuously challenge students and not fall into the practice of lowering expectations. Differentiating instruction plays a key role in setting high expectations because it is instruction that is rigorous, relevant, flexible, varied, and complex (Heacox, 2012). By changing the level, pace, or model of instruction used in delivering content, teachers can respond to the particular needs and interests of students.

Culturally Relevant Instructional Practices

Utilizing the knowledge, skills, and values that students bring into the classroom is teaching with students' strengths in mind. The classroom culture might also call for the need to teach cognitive strategies such as self-questioning and self-reflection, or incorporate cooperative learning strategies. There might be instances where using technology to enhance instruction is necessary. All of these practices are essential components of culturally relevant instruction.

Supporting Parent and Community Involvement

Inviting parents, family, and community members into the classroom and involving them in student learning is a way to help build relationships outside of the school building. It is also a way to expand the learning experience beyond the confines of the classroom. Parents and community members should be viewed as experts in various topic areas; inviting them to engage in the learning process with students will add significant meaning to the ways in which students view the relevancy of content information.

These strategies provide ways for teachers to show students that teachers care about who students are as people, and respect the diverse elements that they bring into the classroom. Incorporating these strategies shows students that teachers care about them as individuals and want to provide the best for them academically.

In order to connect with and build relationships with diverse learners, teachers must learn about their individual needs and show that they care about what their students need to succeed. Students have an innate ability to sense when teachers truly care about helping them meet their needs; caring about students opens the door to teaching content material. Consider the strategies in chapter two, five and eight, as effective ways to build the trusting relationship that is a critical first step for teachers, parents and students.

TEACHING CONTENT WITH PEDAGOGICAL APPROACHES IN MIND

Teaching content involves much more than subject matter, although it is common for teachers to focus on *what* they are teaching over *how* they are doing it at times. Although it is important for teachers to have significant knowledge of content material, teaching subject matter involves more than simply telling students what they need to know. It is an intricate process of melding curriculum content and instructional practices. Three pedagogical approaches, or models of teaching, are used to deliver content information to students: transmission model, generative model, and transformative model (Wink, 2011).

Students who have positive relationships with teachers and peers, and who are engaged, will learn more in the classroom environment. The teaching and learning approach, or model of teaching, in the classroom also impacts student learning. Moving from a more traditional approach, or transmission model, to generative or transformative models allows students to have the opportunity to be more actively involved in the content being taught.

Transmission Model of Teaching

In the transmission model, lessons are teacher-directed, meaning that the teacher is responsible for transmitting knowledge and information. In this model, it is typical for the teacher to present content while positioned at the front of the classroom, in a lecture format. Students are seated in desks and are expected to absorb the content information, usually through note taking. The teacher plays the most active role in this model of teaching.

Generative Model of Teaching

The generative model allows students to take a more active role in learning by working in groups and engaging in exploration. Students are actively engaged in the learning process and must come together to construct knowledge and create meaning. They are able to use new ideas and previous knowledge to generate meaning. Students are active participants in their own learning while the teacher structures and guides classroom experiences (Wink, 2011). This model is beneficial for students as it allows for collaboration and investigation; students can learn by "doing."

Transformative Model of Teaching

The transformative model allows students to participate in authentic activities in the real-world environment. The goal of this model is to continue generating knowledge while extending the learning environment from the classroom to the community (Wink, 2011). Students continue to actively engage in learning and construction of knowledge, but they do so through exploration. The teacher becomes a partner with students in the learning process as meaningful teaching and understanding occurs. The transformative model seeks to prepare students for real-world experiences that they will encounter in the future; it is the most active approach to learning. The goal of the transformative model of teaching is that learning will generate knowledge and extend from the classroom into the community (Wink, 2011, p. 24). Teacher, parent, student, and peer relationships are essential to the transformative model of teaching.

BASIC PRINCIPLES OF TRANSFORMATIVE TEACHING

There are three principles that teachers can use as a platform to build goals that will help them in moving toward transformative teaching. Slavich and Zimbardo (2012) identify these three principles as follows: (1) facilitate students' acquisition and mastery of key course concepts; (2) enhance students' strategies and skills for learning and discovery; and (3) promote positive learning-related attitudes, values, and beliefs in students (p. 10). In a classroom setting, these principles can be addressed in the following ways:

Facilitate Students' Acquisition and Mastery of Key Concepts

- Allow students to work in interdependent teams
  - Share knowledge, responsibility, and ideas, and problem solve together
- Allow students to work at their own pace
- Adapt assignments to match students' interests
- Offer choice
- Increase class time allotted for questioning, debate, role-playing, reflection
- Design assessments that are learning experiences in themselves

Enhance Students' Strategies and Skills for Learning and Discovery

- Think of classrooms as "learning labs"
  - Collaboration between students and teacher
- Provide opportunities to learn by actively engaging in problem solving and discussion
- Share and model tools, strategies, and skills for success with students

Promote Positive Learning-related Attitudes, Values, and Beliefs in Students

- Engage students in collaborative, interdependent problem solving and discussion
  - Discuss and debate ideas
  - Reflect on personal beliefs and alternate points of view

■ Foster dependence on individual capabilities and persistence in order to succeed

With a platform that includes the basic principles of transformative teaching in place, teachers can work toward achieving their transformational teaching goals.

ACHIEVING TRANSFORMATIONAL TEACHING GOALS

Six core strategies can be used as a framework to achieve transformational teaching goals (Slavich & Zimbargo, 2012, p. 14). These strategies include the following:

■ Establishing a shared vision for a course
  ● Work with students to provide a "vision" of what the class, teacher, and students should aim to achieve; envision goals together and work on plans to achieve them
■ Providing modeling and mastery experiences
  ● Train students to apply strategies and skills that are needed to overcome challenges in the learning process (critical thinking, problem solving, collaboration, growth mind-set)
■ Intellectually challenging and encouraging students
  ● Scaffold questions, create class guidelines for communication, and provide time, resources, and support as needed
■ Personalizing attention and feedback
  ● Assess what students know about topics and support them in identifying strengths and weaknesses; help students create an action plan for learning goals
■ Creating experiential lessons that transcend classroom boundaries
  ● Provide opportunities for students to actively construct knowledge and experience content first-hand
■ Promoting ample opportunities for pre-reflection and reflection
  ● Allow time for reflection before and after learning occurs

Classrooms where active learning takes place, allow students to gain better understanding of the material and concepts presented to the class. Too often, teachers do all of the talking while students sit idle. It is especially important for teachers to present content information in ways that will foster critical thinking skills for all students. Ultimately, teachers need to be able to identify the interests, experiences, and ideas of their students in order to engage them in understanding of subject matter. This idea of teacher as facilitator between the student and the curriculum is derived from the work of John Dewey (1938), in which he emphasized the need to connect subject content to students' individual experiences; this is a crucial element in teaching content in a transformational way. Students must be able to make sense of, and personally connect to, what they are being taught. This is where transformation begins to occur, and teachers are the medium through which connections between daily life and content are facilitated.

Ensuring that the learning environment is learner centered and provides for shelter and security, social contact, symbolic interaction, task instrumentality, pleasure, and growth, supports teachers in focusing on all learners in the classroom. From there, teachers can design instruction with pedagogical approaches in mind. The ultimate goal is to plan for transformative teaching by addressing the basic principles and core strategies that are involved in achieving transformative teaching goals. With an understanding of what it means to teach in a transformative environment and knowledge of the elements that contribute to transformative learning opportunities, teachers can begin to plan and implement learning experiences that are life changing.

REFERENCES

Banks, J., Cochran-Smith, M., Moll, L., Richert, A., Zeichner, K., Lepage, P., Darling-Hammond, L., Duffy, H., & McDonald, M. (2005). Teaching diverse learners. In Darling-Hammond, L., & Bransford, J. (Eds.), *Preparing teachers for a changing world: What teachers should learn and be able to do* (pp. 232–274). San Francisco, CA: Jossey-Bass.

Commins, N., & Miramontes, O. (2006). Addressing linguistic diversity from the outset. *Journal of Teacher Education, 57*(3), 240–246.

Dewey, J. (1938). *Education and experience.* New York, NY: Kappa Delta Pi.

Finley, T. (2014, September 2). Helping diverse learners succeed [Blog Post]. Retrieved from edutopia.org/blog/helping-diverse-learners-succeed-todd-finley

Garrett, T. (2014). *Effective classroom management: The essentials.* New York, NY: Teachers College Press.

Hayes Jacobs, H. (2010). *Curriculum 21: Essential education for a changing world.* Alexandria, VA: ASCD.

Heacox, D. (2012). *Differentiating instruction in the regular classroom.* Minneapolis, MN: Free Spirit.

Huba, M., & Freed, J. (2000). *Learner-centered assessment on college campuses: Shifting the focus from teaching to learning.* Needham Heights, MA: Allyn & Bacon.

Slavich, G., & Zimbardo, P. (2012). Transformational teaching: Theoretical underpinnings, basic principles, and core methods. *Educational Psychology, 24*(4), 569–608.

Steele, F. (1973). *Physical settings and organization development.* Reading, MA: Addison-Wesley.

Weinstein, C., & Novodvorsky, I. (2015). *Middle and secondary classroom management: Lessons from research and practice* (5th ed.). New York, NY: McGraw Hill.

Wink, J. (2011). *Critical pedagogy: Notes from the real world* (4th ed.). Upper Saddle River, NJ: Pearson.

PART 1

Lesson Theme:

-

Essential Questions: *List the questions that provide the content and direction for the lesson—these should be large questions that promote exploration, contemplation, and multiple perspectives.*

-

-

-

-

Big Idea: *Write a statement that identifies the most important learning of the unit (overall desired outcome).*

-

PART 2

Principles of Transformative Teaching:

How will you facilitate students' acquisition and mastery of key concepts?

-

-

How will you enhance students' strategies and skills for learning and discovery?

-

-

How will you promote positive learning-related attitudes, values, and beliefs in students?

-

-

Achieving Transformational Teaching Goals: *Describe an action plan that you can put in place for each goal to ensure that the goal is met within the lesson.*

Establish a shared vision-

-

-

Provide modeling and mastery experiences-

-

-

Intellectually challenge and encourage students-

-
-

Personalize attention and feedback-

-
-

Create experiential lessons that transcend classroom boundaries-

-
-

Promote ample opportunities for pre-reflection and reflection-

-
-

ACTIVITY

Transformative Teaching

- Return to the learning experience that you reflected on at the beginning of this chapter. It is likely that many factors involved in transformative teaching were present in that lesson.

ACTIVITY

- Now, think about a content lesson that you might teach in the future. Use the following organizer to help you lay the groundwork necessary in order for you to teach your own transformative lesson.

Differentiation— Relationship-Based Instruction

Contributed by Marci Glessner
©Kendall Hunt Publishing

This chapter focuses on how developing powerful relationships with your students and their parents influences student learning. This chapter will help you understand the following:

- The "why" of differentiation
- How to plan for differentiation based on prior knowledge, experiences, and interest
- How to share your teaching ideas with parents and help engage them as partners in their child's learning

Part One:

- Getting to Know Your Students
- Thinking About How Students Learn

Part Two:

- Designing Instruction With Learners in Mind
- Diagnostic Assessment
- Scaffolding and Extending—Based on Needs
- Choice Cards
- Grouping

INTRODUCTION

As safe and supportive environments are contributing factors to student success and high levels of productivity, it is important for teachers to develop a trusting relationship with students and their families. The foundation for building relationships can be found within the six functions of the classroom setting as described in the previous chapter. A school setting that provides security and shelter while also applying elements of social contact, symbolic identification, task instrumentality, pleasure, and growth, builds relationships and engages learners – allowing for differentiated instruction and supports that meet the individual needs of those they serve.

There are many ways to think about differentiation and how it is a part of our everyday lives. Authors Gregory and Chapman (2007) discussed how clothes are not sold as "one size" fits all. Rather, there are numerous styles and sizes and options available for our differing tastes and bodies. The same holds true for grocery shopping. Many options are available, starting with deciding whether or not you want to browse the store yourself or enlist the help of an online shopper, followed by the act of choosing the size of cart necessary for your grocery run. We can choose to carry our bags to our car, or have them loaded right into the backseat, or even have them delivered to our home. The commercialized world has learned that in order to be successful it needs to adapt and provide options for all kinds of shoppers; we, in education, need to do the same when thinking about the students in our classrooms. We are long past the time when one could assume our students came to our classrooms with similar backgrounds and learning experiences, and that they learned the same way and at the same rate. Each student is an individual with many unique gifts to share. Therefore, the idea of building relationships with students and their families, as well as getting to know them as learners, is at the core of differentiation.

PART 1: KNOWING OUR STUDENTS

Having a sense of who our students "are" is important for all learners, yet it is vitally important for those who have typically been disenfranchised by local and global communities. Moll, Amanti, Neff and Gonzalez (1992) highlight the idea of understanding children's "funds of knowledge" and incorporating that understanding into our teaching. Funds of knowledge, in general terms, refers to the social and historical learning, skills and knowledge that comes from within the family or household. It is, in a sense, a bank of coping mechanisms a child first learns in order to navigate their world. As we work with our students, it is imperative we learn about these funds of knowledge and subsequently integrate them into our everyday classroom learning and experiences. This can be accomplished through family involvement.

One way to foster involvement is to invite families into the child's learning by exploring varying routes that include all families. Chapter five provided a variety of events and opportunities that may contribute to the development relationships and, ultimately, partnership. Examples included a typical "Open House" at the beginning of the school year where children come see the classroom with their families in tow, a visit to each child's home before the beginning of the school year, or asking parents to share their favorite book with the class (via an in-person visit or a recording of their reading). Communication such as a personal email exchanges, telephone calls, an app, or a notebook going back and forth between home and school are also tools to use that help parents make and maintain contact with the school setting and their child's teachers.

Learning about our student's funds of knowledge doesn't stop with the parents. Within the classroom there are a variety of methods we can use to learn even more: informal conversation, student reading or writing conferences, interest inventories, learning styles and multiple intelligence surveys. Each of these strategies or tools can provide insight into a child and/or family.

Informal Conversation

Visits to a grocery store rarely end without learning something about other shoppers. An idea for supper can occur through a happenstance glance into a fellow shopper's grocery cart and noticing a cut of salmon beside a package of cedar planks.

Shoppers often stop in front of a bin of produce, each taking time to find the perfectly ripe tomato or avocado—sharing tips with others if asked. Conversation and recommendations happen in the aisles and in the checkout lanes. Informal conversations such as these highlight the value of conversation in our everyday learning experiences.

A few minutes here and there, talking to strangers at the grocery store helps build relationships and develop culinary skills, as noted above. Talking with students for a few minutes, scattered throughout the school day, helps educators reflect on their teaching and student learning, ultimately helping students develop as learners. Take advantage of any down time to be present with your students. Examples of such times include the morning greeting, snack time, those few minutes during transitions between subjects, time spent monitoring the lunch line or recess, and as the day wraps up. The conversation doesn't have to be mind-blowing – it just needs to be a part of the day in which you enjoy listening to what the kids have to say, what they feel is important, and what they notice.

Student Conferences

Reading and writing workshops have long been a core of literacy teaching (Anderson, 2000; Atwell, 1987; Fletcher & Portalupi, 2001; Hagerty, 1992; Hindley, 1996; Yates & Nosek, 2018). Part of what works so well with the workshop approach is the student conferences that are held each day as part of students' framework. These conferences consist of individually meeting with students about their work with reading and writing. There isn't a set agenda to the conference, just conversation which then leads the teacher toward further teaching opportunities. In fact, conferences have been referred to as the "heart" of reading and writing workshops.

Although student conferences may feel more formal than informal conversations, they are an excellent way to touch base with students about academics and their interests, work habits, and communication styles. By sitting with a child at least once a week for 5 minutes in a reading or writing conference, a teacher will have spent almost 3 hours in a one-on-one sitting with that student over the course of a school year; this, of course, doesn't account for all the other times throughout the day a teacher might spend with the student. Just think about the things we will discover about the student and how we might use that knowledge to further engage the student in other learning.

Student Interest Inventories

Numerous published interest inventories exist; perform a Google search of "interest inventory elementary" and over 1,840,000 hits pop up. Rather than pull one published inventory from the Internet, it makes more sense to think about what you, as the classroom teacher, want to know about your students. Do you want to know what they enjoy doing in their free time? What they like to read? How they feel about science? How much TV they watch? What do they want to be when they grow up? Please bear in mind the purpose of the interest inventory isn't to judge our students, nor their parents; it is to begin, develop, and sustain relationships with our students and their families. In chapter two we discussed the creation of a student or a family questionnaire, based on what you might find helpful as you work on constructing meaningful conversations. Keep in mind that you may want to create a student interest inventory or a student questionnaire multiple times a year with different questions that help you to better understand what you can't always see. This information can start conversations with families and even provide moments of lightheartedness during times that may otherwise be stressful, as the following example illustrates.

When our oldest daughter was younger she had a hard time falling asleep at night and no amount of pleading, cajoling, or home remedies seemed to help. One day, as they were learning about home addresses, her preschool teacher asked her where she lived. Sophie's response was, "An old house with cracks in the ceiling." As a result, the teacher found out we lived in a 100-year-old home with a looping crack right above Sophie's bed. She also realized that Sophie noticed that crack every single night as she struggled falling asleep—information her teacher had not been aware of. We laughed about Sophie's response during parent–teacher conferences, but this exchange also provided us with an opportunity to share our concern about her sleeping habits with her teacher, and why Sophie may have had difficulty falling asleep at night.

The key is, as we know more about our students, we can better incorporate those funds of knowledge into our teaching. Below you will find a sampling of questions you might consider using in a student interest survey or a student questionnaire.

If you are waiting at the doctor's office or a bus station, how do you pass the time?

What do you want to be when you grow up?

What's the title of the last book you read? Did you enjoy it? Why or why not?

What are two things you like to do during any free time you have?

What is one thing you would change about school?

What is the primary language spoken in your home?

Siblings? Grandparents? Cousins? Aunts and Uncles?

Who is someone you look up to, like to spend time with?

Where do you live?

Are you a breakfast eater? What's your favorite breakfast food?

What is your bedtime routine? Your morning routine?

Sample Interest Inventory Questions (Glessner, 2019)

Learning Style Inventories

Since the 1960s, educators have commonly utilized teaching practices focused on reaching all students by determining the learning styles of students in a given classroom and incorporating a variety of modalities (auditory, visual, kinesthetic) into their teaching (Farid & Abbasi, 2014). The premise behind this was that we could better reach our students if we were teaching to the way they learned best. For example, educators often believe a person who is a visual learner will better understand information if they read about it.

In 2008, a group of researchers critically studied the existing research on learning styles and improvement in student learning, only to find there is little scientific backing to this common teaching practice (Pashler, McDaniel, Rohrer, & Bjork, 2008). A follow-up study conducted with college-educated adults was then undertaken, with the results also highlighting a lack of statistically significant evidence to support the idea that providing instruction in a learner's preferred modality will result in better learning (Rogowsky, Calhoun, & Tallal, 2014).

Bear in mind, however, this does not mean that anecdotal evidence is not in existence to support the idea of learning styles. Both children and adults do, when asked, often state a preferred learning style and may demonstrate strengths with processing information shared (Pashler, McDaniel, Rohrer, & Bjork, 2008). What does this mean to future educators? It means we can observe and develop an understanding of any or all of the following as we provide optimal learning environments, present content through multiple modalities, and provide options for students to access and demonstrate their learning.

Who likes to learn with a partner?
Who would prefer to gain new information through reading?
Who always walks around as they are telling a story?
Who benefits from taking frequent breaks?
Who can concentrate no matter the volume of the classroom?
Where, in the classroom, does Jazmin like to study?
When given a choice, how does D'Shane prefer to demonstrate their learning?

Multiple Intelligences

In 1983, Gardner proposed the theory of multiple intelligences—suggesting there is more than one way to learn and express that learning. At that time many schools fit the "one size fits all" mode of teaching. Teachers lectured at the front of the classroom while students listened, then modeled the process of solving a problem or figuring out an unknown word. Students then practiced the skill or strategy with teacher guidance, and all completed the same assignment—whether or not they struggled with the concept or if they already knew the concept and could finish the assignment in a matter of minutes. Gardner (1983) believed there are many ways to gain knowledge, although there are also many ways to express knowledge. The eight multiple intelligences, interrelated yet individual, are depicted in the table below.

Multiple Intelligence	Description
Interpersonal	Works well in a group setting—learns from self and others, cooperative
Intrapersonal	Thinks within themselves, self-reflective, requires individual processing time
Bodily/Kinesthetic	Learns through movement, using body, touch, sensory, action
Visual	Learns though visual means—reading, watching, observing
Musical	Learns though music, patterns, and rhythms
Logical/Mathematical	Analytic mind—order, logic, spacing, patterns, and sequence, abstract
Naturalistic	Sees sense in nature, the natural state of being, organic, growth in transition, sorting, classifying
Verbal/Linguistic	Good with words—oral (speaking and listening), reading, and writing

As we begin to discover the interests and the learning styles of our students, we then must then contemplate how to use the information that we have gathered. It is important you don't just see a child as a "logical/mathematical thinker" to the exclusion of their other areas of strength (and/or weaknesses). Rather, use this information to create a learning environment where students become risk-takers, are engaged in learning, and are confident in themselves and their abilities.

What to Do With This Information?

Learner Profile Cards

As information about our students (who they like to work with, what kinds of activities they are naturally drawn to, what their reading levels are, who they work well with, what their interests are, and so forth) is gathered, it can be complied into a student profile card, which can then be referenced as instructional decisions are made.

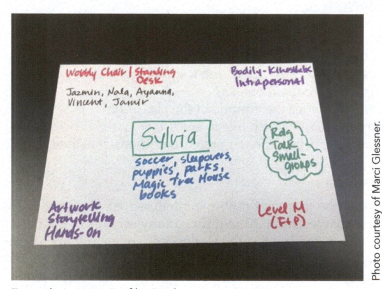

Photo courtesy of Marci Glessner.

Example Learner Profile Card

"Sylvia's" interests are clear as they are noted below her name. Her preferred sitting spot and partners are highlighted in the top left corner, whereas her two highest-scoring multiple intelligences are in the top right corner. On the bottom left, the teacher has noted Sylvia prefers to demonstrate her learning through artwork, hands-on activities, or storytelling, whereas the bottom right highlights her current reading level. As information on each student in the classroom is collected, a Class Profile can ultimately be created.

These tools, together, are powerful as they can be referenced as the classroom teacher plans for grouping decisions (whole group, small group, or partners). They can also serve as a reminder that not all students learn in the same manner or at the same time.

Class Learning Profile (Glessner, 2019)
Teacher: _____   Grade: _____
Academic
Put each student's initials in the corresponding box.

Gathering Knowledge	Area of Strength	Area of Weakness
Gathers knowledge through reading	A, C, ED	
Gathers knowledge through discussing	A, C, ED	EB
Gathers knowledge through listening	S*	
Gathers knowledge through games/interactions	H, S*, M, EB, C	ED
Gathers knowledge through observation and/or videos	A, EB, C, ED, L, K, S*	
Gathers knowledge through textbooks, worksheets	C, ED	H, S*, M, L, A, EB
Gathers knowledge through computer, Internet reading	C, ED	EB
Gathers knowledge through small group or 1:1 assistance	H, S*, K, L, A, EB	

References "Sylvia" – the student from the example learner profile card previously shared

Demonstrating Knowledge	Area of Strength	Area of Need
Demonstrates knowledge through writing (paper/pencil, journal, reports)	H, C, ED	M, L, S*, A, EB
Demonstrates knowledge through physical demonstration (manipulatives, acting out)	M, L, S*, H, C, EB	ED
Demonstrates knowledge through oral discussion (book club discussion, debate, interview)	M, L, S*, EB, K, H	
Demonstrates knowledge through presentation or projects (drawing, diagramming, book report, video demonstration)	A, C, ED, H, S*	M, L
Demonstrates knowledge through tests or textbook exercises	H, C, ED, A	M, L, S*, H

References "Sylvia" – the student from the example learner profile card previously shared

Social/Behavorial
Put each student's initials in the corresponding box.

Preferred Manner of Receiving Knowledge	
Alone	L, H,
Partner	K
Small Group	H, S*, K, L, A, EB, C, ED
Whole Group	H, C, ED
Computer/Technology	H, S*, M, L, C

References "Sylvia" – the student from the example learner profile card previously shared

Preferred Work Setting	
Alone	L, H, S*
Partner	M, C
Small Group	S*, A, C, ED
Whole Group	H, C, ED
Computer/Technology	H, S*, M, L, C
Teacher-Led Small Group	H, S*, K, L, A, EB

References "Sylvia" – the student from the example learner profile card previously shared

Example Class Profile

ACTIVITY

Learner Profile Card

Create learner profile card on yourself—complete with your preferred methods of learning, your strengths in regard to multiple intelligences, and partner preferences. As you prepare to co-teach, share it with your teaching partner. How are the two of you similar? How are you different? What might this mean for your teaching experience?

PART TWO: DESIGNING INSTRUCTION WITH LEARNERS IN MIND

So, what purpose does knowing our students have if we don't utilize that information in our everyday teaching? None. As daily lessons are planned it is imperative we make use of all the tools we have to reach all our students; we need to design our instruction with our students in mind.

To begin, think of the end goal for student learning. At the end of a particular unit or lesson, what are students expected to know and be able to demonstrate? What do they already know about the topic? What are gaps in their knowledge that need to be worked with before the larger concept learning can occur?

For the purpose of this chapter and its examples, we will look at the "unit" level of learning—in keeping with the grocery theme, we'll work with a health unit: "Making Healthy Eating Choices."

Diagnostic Assessment

Before going grocery shopping, shoppers take inventory of their pantry and create a list. What staples are running low? What's on the menu this week? Any new ingredients that are needed?

It doesn't do much good to come home from the grocery store only to realize you already had two pints of cream in the refrigerator. Likewise, in a classroom we want to know where our students are in the learning process. The purpose of a diagnostic assessment, or preassessment, is to gather information regarding what students already know about an upcoming topic of study. By having a sense of students' background knowledge and experience, educators can begin the topic at the students' levels of understanding and build on what they know. There isn't one correct way to create a diagnostic assessment; the key is there is one. Examples of a diagnostic assessment for the health unit may include the following:

- a picture of a grocery cart full of a variety of food, with space below for students to write down what know about healthy food and to sort foods into categories
- a multiple-choice test regarding healthy eating concepts
- a list of statements about foods and healthy eating—students state if they agree or disagree with each statement
- a list of food-related vocabulary—students write the definitions

The diagnostic assessment is given to each student, ideally at least a week or so before the unit begins so adaptations to teaching and learning opportunities, as needed, can be made. When conducting the assessment, ensure students understand this is a tool that will help the teacher learn about them—it is not graded, nor are they expected to know all the answers. If a child is not able to independently complete the diagnostic assessment, the same tool can be used, but do ensure accommodations are provided (such as reading the questions to the child and allowing oral answers) as we want to know what the child does know about the topic, not that reading is difficult.

After the assessment has been administered, teacher reflection comes into play. Look for patterns and themes among the student answers. What knowledge do all students already possess? What are concepts that only a few students knew, or mentioned? What misconceptions are present? Armed with this information, we can plan the unit and/or individual lessons. One of the first places to begin is to create a tiered learning grid, based on this diagnostic assessment.

Scaffolding and Extending, Based on Needs

Differentiation occurs within a unit of study, as well as with individual lessons. To begin, we must look at the overarching learning standard or target. What is the expectation for student learning? Once this is in place we can take a look at students and their learning, based on the results of the diagnostic assessment and create a tiered learning grid. Who needs more background before the understanding of the standard can occur? What kind of background knowledge is needed? How can teaching the background knowledge be provided? Who is "right where they should be" as far as the learning? Who already demonstrates knowledge of the learning target?

Through the creation of a tiered learning grid like the one highlighted below, educators are able to see the entire scope of students, their learning, and their background knowledge. What content can be briefly reviewed before addressing the bigger concepts? What gaps need to be filled? From this point, teachers can determine the focus of future lessons and plan for teaching approaches that will work best in this situation. For example, would it work best to use a Choice Card (see next section) and have station teaching in the classroom? With this choice of teaching approach, students would work independently, but it would still provide time for a teacher to work with individuals or small groups of students on focused lessons. Would it be best to teach lessons as a whole group and then move toward small group or partner work? Or, for some students, does it make sense to use a Learning Contract so they can work at their own pace while still ensuring they understand the content and are able to expand the depth and breadth of their understanding?

Learning Target: What is the grade level expectation/standard?		
Approaching: *Students who need more scaffolding* *What might that scaffolding look like?*	**Meeting:** *Students who have some background knowledge of the topic and are "right where we want them."* *What teaching is needed?*	**Exceeding:** *Students who already demonstrate an understanding of the learning target.* *What extensions may work for these learners?*
What information does the student already know? Is that knowledge literal knowledge or inferential knowledge? What skills or strategies need to be taught? What supports can be offered to ensure access? How do they learn best? How can they access and demonstrate learning?	What skills or strategies need to be taught? How do they learn best? How can they access and demonstrate learning?	What information does the child already know? Is it inferential knowledge? What concepts can be taught to extend the learning? How do they learn best? How can they access and demonstrate learning?

Tiered Learning Grid: Questions to Reflect Upon

Differentiation within an individual lesson most often occurs in terms of accommodations or modifications to the lesson in the form of scaffolding the learning, but we must not forget to also extend the learning for those who have already mastered key content information. Again, knowing our students is key to differentiation. By using a tiered grid like the one above, but this time for an individual lesson objective, educators are able to reflect on how to best meet the needs of their students. A tiered learning grid can also be useful in developing a menu of learning opportunities in the form of a choice card.

Choice Cards

A Choice Card provides a path for students to select activities of interest to them, building or deepening their knowledge of the overarching content as they complete learning activities. The activities are based on the diagnostic information and carefully selected with individual learners in mind. A key to successful implementation of a choice card is that students must be familiar with each of the learning activities so their focus is on the content learning and they do not get stuck on how to complete an activity, or choice.

Choice Card Example

Topic: Healthy Eating

Directions: Complete the center box. Then, choose two other activities to create a tic-tac-toe.

Read _The Vegetables We Eat, by Gail Gibbons_. After reading, write down five facts you learned about vegetables.	**Create a healthy plate.** Using pictures from a magazine, cut out healthy food choices. Glue them to a paper plate.	**Pick five healthy foods; list them.** Describe how would you cook and serve them. Create a new recipe using all five foods.
Pick two recipes from the cookbook _Eat Your Greens, Reds, Yellows and Purples_. Write a note to the main "chef" at your house stating why you'd like these items served at a meal and listing three reasons they are healthy.	**Food journal:** Keep track of everything you eat for 2 days. This includes anything you put in your mouth (even gum).	**Watch the animated video about vegetables.** Make a list of three to five veggies you enjoy and how you like to eat them (cooked, steamed, raw, and so forth). https://youtu.be/RE5tvaveVak
Look at an ad from a grocery store. Compare prices on healthy and nonhealthy food. Write about your findings. Which is more expensive? What does this mean to you as a shopper?	**Read _Gregory the Terrible Eater_, by Mitchell Sharmat.** List foods you regularly eat that might be considered "terrible." Come up with one alternative food for each of the "terrible" ones.	**Pick three food items from the grocery cart in the classroom.** Read the labels on each and determine how big one serving of the food is. Of the three items, write about the ones you would find to be the most filling or satisfying.

Glessner (2019)

Example Choice Card

There is not one way to prepare a Choice Card—it should be as individual as the students in the class. The activities should provide for different levels of understanding and varying degrees of difficulty in regard to task completion. Check out the options above and using that information, think about the varying types of learners who might be present within that classroom.

The Choice Card above includes a "Must Do" activity—this activity can be thought of as a measuring stick by which to gauge student understanding. There are two ways of thinking about this: a teacher can decide to have students complete the "Must Do" after the required number of activities are completed as a "capstone" of sorts, or students can complete it before beginning the Choice Card activities, as a way to ensure everyone gains a bit of background knowledge of the topic before beginning individual work.

As an educator, you are certainly not limited to these types of activities. They may form the base of a Choice Card from year to year, but the activities should change to reflect the group dynamic. For example, if, in the future, a group of students loves Readers' Theatre and putting on plays, then why not have one of the choices be either preparing a Readers' Theatre script about eating healthy or recording a script? If students write the script they are extending their knowledge of healthy eating—whereas other students who read an already-prepared script will gain a basic understanding of food facts.

Choice Cards are not meant to be the end of your planning for differentiation—in fact, they can be viewed as just one component to a well-rounded differentiated plan. They may provide the backbone of your unit plan, but educators must also think about how students might go about completing learning activities.

Grouping

As mentioned earlier, educators have a choice in planning for and arranging grouping situations within their classrooms. Gone are the days when all teaching was done in front of the classroom, lecture style; it has been replaced by flexible grouping options that occur throughout the school day. Gregory and Chapman (2007) suggest using the acronym TAPS to help educators think about the varying options for group work: total group, alone, partners, or small group.

As with any teaching, it is important to determine the group configuration that is best used to engage students in the learning process. Although it is tempting to fall into a routine and use just one style, variety is wonderful as it provides opportunities for students to share information in differing settings. It provides voice to all students.

Grouping Option	Description
Total	Best used to convey the same information to everyone. The key is to ensure all students are engaged in the learning.
Alone	Some students prefer to work by themselves, and they should at times be given opportunities to do so.
Partner	Provides more autonomy as the partners can direct their own learning. Be careful that one student doesn't overtake the learning experience.
	It is important to ensure that a child who is exceeding the learning expectations is not always placed with a child who is approaching them. Mix it up.
Small Group	Heterogeneous or homogeneous—flexible and depends on the reason for grouping the students. Do you want children of the same ability to all work together, or would you prefer to have a mixed-ability group?
	Provides an opportunity for the classroom teacher to focus on a small group of 3 to 5 students at a time. Students who are quieter may have a chance to share in a small group, whereas they may feel overwhelmed in the whole class setting.

With all types of learning situations, educators must be present during the learning process—monitoring, checking for understanding, and helping extend thinking. Groups should be determined based on the task at hand and be thoughtfully arranged so the best outcome for learning is possible.

SUMMARY

Differentiation is much like grocery shopping—even as each shopper has the same goal in mind (to purchase food), no one person's shopping experience will be like another's. In education, although we may have a learning target in mind there are many ways for students to access the topic and many ways for them to demonstrate learning. Start with the students in the classroom, the students who are right in front of you, learn from them, and you'll be off to a wonderful beginning.

BOOKS ON DIFFERENTIATION

1. *Do-Able Differentiation, by Michael F. Opitz and Michael Ford*
2. *Co-Teaching in the Differentiated Classroom (Grade 5 to 8),* by Melinda L. Fattig and Maureen Tormey Taylor

3. *Differentiating for the Young Child, Teaching Strategies Across the Content Areas, PreK-3*, by Joan Franklin Smutny and S. E. Von Fremd

4. *Making Differentiation a Habit*, by Diane Heacox

REFERENCES

Anderson, C. (2000). *How's it going: A practical guide to conferring with student writers*. Portsmouth, NH: Heinemann.

Atwell, N. (1987). *In the Middle: Writing, Reading and Learning with Adolescents*. Portsmouth, NH: Heinemann.

Farid, S., & Abbasi, S. (2014). Learning styles: History, conceptualization and continuum. *Social Sciences Review, 2*, 15–31.

Fletcher, R., & Portalupi, J. (2001). *Writing workshop: The essential guide*. Portsmouth, NH: Heinemann.

Gardner, H. (1983). *Multiple intelligences: The theory into practice*. New York, NY: BasicBooks.

Gregory, G. H., & Chapman, C. (2007). *Differentiated instructional strategies: One size doesn't fit all* (2nd ed.). Thousand Oaks, CA: Corwin Press.

Hagerty, P. (1992). *Readers' workshop: Real reading*. Ontario, Canada: Scholastic Canada, Ltd.

Hindley, J. (1996). *In the company of children*. Portland, ME: Stenhouse.

Learning styles debunked: There is no evidence supporting auditory and visual learning, psychologists say. (December 16, 2009). *Association for Psychological Science*. Retrieved from https://www.psychologicalscience.org/news/releases/learning-styles-debunked-there-is-no-evidence-supporting-auditory-and-visual-learning-psychologists-say.html

Moll, L. C., Amanti, C., Neff, D., & Gonzalez, N. (1992). Funds of knowledge for teaching: Using a qualitative approach to connect homes and classrooms. *Theory Into Practice, 31*, 132–141.

Pashler, H., McDaniel, M., Rohrer, D., & Bjork, R. (2008). Learning styles: Concepts and evidence. *Psychological Science in the Public Interest, 9*, 105–119.

Rogowsky, B., Calhoun, B., & Tallal, P. (2014). Matching learning style to instructional method: Effects on comprehension. *Journal of Educational Psychology, 107*, 64–78.

Yates, K., & Nosek, C. (2018). *To know and nurture a reader: Conferring with confidence and joy*. Portland, ME: Stenhouse.

Getting to Know the Child and Sharing Your Perspective With Parents

- How will you go about knowing your students' strengths and areas of need?

- How will you share this information with parents? How can you use them as a resource for your information gathering?

- What is your experience with differentiation? How did it help or hinder your learning process?

ACTIVITY

Differentiation Lesson

- Highlight five students in a classroom—design a differentiated lesson that meets all of their needs. To do so, think about the areas of strength/weaknesses of each student. How can you ensure access to the content is provided to each student?

Appendix A

Administrative Parent Partnership Assessment and Action Plan		
District:	School:	School leader:
In what way do school leaders currently create an environment that welcomes parents in our schools?		
In what ways do school leaders currently model a relationship-based school environment?		
In what ways does the administration currently support the building of parent–teacher partnerships?		
What training or resources might the teachers need to advance the development of parent–teacher partnerships?		
Administrative goals to advance the development of relationship-based parent–teacher collaboration		
Goal 1: Who	Will do what?	By When?
Goal 2: Who	Will do what?	By When?

Transformative Education, by Ritland 2019. Kendall-Hunt Publishing Co.

Appendix B

Faculty/Staff Parent Partnership Assessment and Action Plan		
What do we currently do to create an environment that welcomes parents in our classroom?		
In what ways do we currently model relationship-based parent–teacher partnerships?		
What training or additional resources might teachers need to further develop parent–teacher partnerships?		
Acknowledging that research substantiates that parent–teacher partnerships have positive outcomes for students, teachers, and schools, what more are we willing to do to partner with parents?		
Goal 1: Who	Will do what?	By When? Resources needed?
Goal 2: Who	Will do what?	By When? Resources needed?
District:	School:	Teachers participating in assessment plan:

Transformative Education, by Ritland, 2019. Kendall-Hunt Publishing Co.

Appendix C
Parent Partnership Plan

Type of involvement	Describe (NOT LIST) the activities or strategies that would address this area. Number each of your strategies. There should be a corresponding number in column 3 to align with each strategy. Identify two ideas for each area.	Describe the preparation or training needed to ensure a successful experience for parents for each strategy. (You should have something to address each of your strategies and the numbers should align.)
Type I. Parenting: Help all families establish home environments to support children as students.		
Type II. Communicating: Design effective forms of school-to-home communications about school programs and children's progress.		
Type III. Volunteering: Recruit and organize parent help and support.		

Type IV. Learning at home: Provide information and ideas to families about how to help students at home with homework and other curriculum-related activities, decisions, and planning.		
Type V. Decision-making: Include parents in school decisions, developing parent leaders and representatives.		
Type VI. Collaboration with the community: Identify and integrate resources and services from the community to strengthen school programs, family practices, and student learning and development.		

Appendix D
Guidelines on How to Develop a Family Questionnaire

INTRODUCTION PAGE OF FAMILY QUESTIONNAIRE

If you are asking families for information to help you get to know their child/family, then it is only fair that you share a bit about yourself as well. Therefore, you should attach an introduction letter to your family questionnaire document that includes the following:

- At least one paragraph on who you are as a teacher
- One paragraph explaining the rationale for the questionnaire (Why are you asking these questions? What is the purpose of this document?)
- A closing paragraph/statement that thanks them for completing the document and includes your name and email address if they should have questions
- A graphic, your picture or something, added to this introduction page to make it interesting and inviting to the parent. One-inch margins are recommended for the letter (more or less if you have included a border)

QUESTIONNAIRE

- Consider adding graphics or a friendly font in your document to create interest.
- Use ½-inch margins for your questionnaire to **maximize** writing space.
- At the top of the questionnaire document, write a **few sentences** about rationale for this document; include your name so that if the letter gets separated from your questionnaire, the parents know where the document came from. Let them know they are welcome to omit any questions they are uncomfortable answering.
- Be sure to have a place on your tool for the child's name and a line for who completed this questionnaire.
- Don't be afraid to take some risks with some of your questions. You are not trying to pry but you want to understand the child and how this family functions.
- Avoid yes or no, or dead-end questions. Ask **open-ended questions**.
- Leave **adequate room** for them to respond to your questions, but also avoid excessive white space between paragraphs or at the end of your document. If you find you have extra white space at the end of your document, go back and add another question or two.
- Don't start a question on one page and continue the question on the next page, or have their writing space go onto the next page.

- Ask yourself what information you can gather from the parent that will help you understand the child and the family.

- What questions might you ask to understand the culture of the family or how the family functions?

- Divide your document into **two** sections: **questions about the child** and **questions about the family**. You should have approximately seven to eight quality questions in each section.

- It is the intent of this tool that a parent or parents will respond to the child and family questions, so your questions should be written with that in mind.

- Avoid asking questions that provide information you can find in the child's file or the health history form (for example: child's birth date; who will drop off or pick up child, who is in the family).

- Depending on graphics, your document will likely be four to six pages long. When handouts get too long, parents tend to avoid completing and returning them.

- Be sure to add a word of thanks at the **bottom of the last page of the document, along with your name and contact information.** Adjust your spacing throughout the document so that you don't leave any extra wasted white space on the last page.

Note: You can also find similar documents available online. Use them as resources to gather ideas. Your family questionnaire should be an instrument that is helpful to you. Design your own tool customized to what you think is most relevant to understanding the children and families you serve.

Transformative Education by Ritland, 2019. Kendall-Hunt Publishing Co.

Appendix E
Analytical Versus Judgmental

Read the situations and then write your response to each situation in **analytical** not judgmental terms. What are the feelings that you might have or the immediate response you would feel to these situations? **Would you say or do anything in these situations; if so, what would you do?**

1. You make a home visit to a family and when you walk in the door the apartment is smoke filled. You are aware that the child in your classroom has severe allergies. You also know that there is a new baby at home.

2. You are working with a family that you know is struggling financially. They are on food stamps and renter's assistance. The family can't afford school supplies, and the three children in the family all come to school not properly dressed for winter and with clothes that don't properly fit. The school recently had a fall fundraising event to help with medical expenses for one of the children who had extensive medical needs. In the spring, one of the children in this family has a birthday, and the family throws an elaborate birthday party. Two limousines pick up the entire class after school (class of 22). Everyone is taken to Skateland for a skating party, and then to Happy Joes for pizza and games. Some estimate this family spent about $400–$500 on the birthday party. What questions or emotions are rising? How do you address the gossip among the families who are curious and even bothered by their observations?

3. Parents never show up for conferences, attend school functions, or ever send anything back that you need signed. How do you feel and what will you do?

4. Your second-grade student often talks about the R-rated movies or horror movies that they watched over the weekend? Should you say or do something, if so what will you do?

5. One of your fourth-grade students comes tardy to school (by 10–15 minutes) 3 or 4 days out of every week. Should you say or do something, if so, what will you do? How do you handle this situation and who should be involved?

Transformative Education by Ritland, 2019. Kendall-Hunt Publishing Co.

Appendix F
Ghosts in the Classroom

Using your story line, identify two significant events or people in your life. Write about them in the middle column. Then fill in the first column and the second column on how those experiences or people might have had a potential positive and a potential negative impact on you as a person and teacher.

What potential negative impact might this "ghost" have on us as a teacher?	What "ghosts" do we bring to the classroom?	What potential positive impact might this "ghost" have on us as a teacher?

Transformative Education, by Ritland, 2019. Kendall-Hunt Publishing Co.

Appendix G

Team Profile
Please complete all areas that you are comfortable sharing with the team.

Issue, problem, or question that the team is addressing:

Team Member	Role on the Team	Email Address	Phone No.:
My perspective of the problem is:			
The strengths, expertise, or skills that I bring to the team are:			

Team Member	Role on the Team	Email Address	Phone No.:
My perspective of the problem is:			
The strengths, expertise, or skills that I bring to the team are:			

Team Member	Role on the Team	Email Address	Phone No.:
My perspective of the problem is:			
The strengths, expertise, or skills that I bring to the team are:			

Transformative Education, by Ritland, 2019. Kendall-Hunt Publishing Co.

Appendix H

Team Meeting Worksheet		
Team Name:		Date of Meeting:
Team Ground Rules:		
Team members present:	Team members absent:	

Team Roles		
Facilitator:	Timekeeper:	Note taker:

Agenda	
Agenda items:	Time limit:
1. Review ground rules and where we left off	
2. Updates on action plan items from last meeting	
3. Old business	
4. New business	
5. Develop action plan/tasks to be completed	
6. Meeting evaluation	

Action Plan		
Task:	Person responsible:	Due date:
1.		
2.		
3.		
4.		

Agenda for Next Meeting		
Date/time:	Facilitator:	Note taker & Timekeeper:
Agenda:		

Appendix I

Collaboration Evaluation Survey			
Establishing Team	**Yes**	**No**	**Comments**
Team developed strategies to build relationships			
Team discussed or considered each member's perspective and their role on the team			
Team established ground rules			
Team identified purpose, goals, and clear direction			
Functioning as Team			
Team complies with the ground rules			
All team members perspectives are considered			
Meetings start and end on time			
Meetings have an agenda and team members are committed to staying on task			
All team members feel safe in contributing to discussion and decisions			
Team has a recorder who writes down outcomes and action items			
Team members follow through on their action items			
Ground rules are reviewed periodically			
Team members are present and on time for meetings			
The team regularly evaluates their meetings and their work			
Conflict is resolved and not ignored			
Other:			
Team goals to address any issues above			

Appendix J
Building Resiliency

Teacher:	District:	Date of Plan:
Ginsburg's Crucial C's of building resiliency:	**What the teacher/school can do to build this skill:**	**What a parent or a mentor can do to build this skill:**
Competency		
Confidence		
Connection		
Character		
Contribution		
Coping		
Control		
Comments/Notes		

Authors Final Reflection
Look Out the Window!

There are windows in our cars, in our homes, in our schools, in our banks, and in other kinds of businesses. When families look for homes, they consider it an asset in their search if there are a lot of windows, with natural light coming in. When the education building at my university was being renovated and we were about to move back in to our new space, faculty with seniority were the first to pick their offices. Everyone with seniority was quick to select the offices that had two windows, over those that had one window. In addition, the classrooms that everyone prefers to teach in are the ones with the most windows. If you look at the architect of new buildings, you might easily identify modern architect by the abundance of windows!

Although most enjoy the presence of windows, it is my observation that where there are windows there are also blinds and curtains to block out the light and the view. Sadly, it is likely that the blinds and curtains are more often closed than they are open. At times I am tempted to shout, open the blinds, look out the window!

My favorite room in my house is my home office. It is the only room in my house where there are no blinds or curtains on my windows. It is the room where I work, where I read, where I think, where I pray, and where my view is not blocked in any way. While there is nothing significant outside of my windows, I do often just sit in my office and stare at the nothingness that is there. Very soon, I began to see what looked like nothing has become very significantly something. The American flag flapping in the wind represents my appreciation for my sons and all those who served and are serving in the military, and that appreciation will move me to tears. My mailbox represents the excitement of the cards and gifts that have been delivered to me in my lifetime, and I am so grateful for the blessings of the family and friends who have sent them. The tree in my back yard was a gift from my in-laws and while they have and will part from this world, the tree will continue to grow and represent life. The flowers and the shrubs outside my window represent the richness of the soil in our Midwest, and they remind me of my years as a child growing up on a farm, planting and harvesting each year the gardens and the fields. The trees and the river in the distance represent the amazing artistic work of our heavenly Father, and they remind me of all of the blessings and challenges he has bestowed on me. I find peace, and strength and wisdom in the nothingness that lies outside my window.

As I summarize what this book is really all about, a good analogy might be to open the blinds and *look out the window.* My caution, however, would be to be careful that we don't look too quickly or too mindlessly. Look out the window each day with the intent to see what is amazing. Look at your children each day to see what is amazing. Look at your parents and colleagues each day and see what is amazing. See the potential, consider the history, get to know the stories, build the relationships, and when we do, the nothingness will become something very significant, indeed!

If we know that working with parents and colleagues in a true *partnership* can increase student outcomes, what are we willing to do? It all begins with building the relationship. I wish you well.

Dr. Valerie Vanyo Ritland